K-2 CHART SENSE

Common Sense Charts to Teach K-2 Informational Text and Literature

Rozlyn Linder, Ph.D.

The Literacy Initiative

Atlanta

K-2 Chart Sense: Common Sense Charts to Teach K-2 Informational Text and Literature

www.ChartSense.RozLinder.com

CHART SENSE and K-2 CHART SENSE are trademarks of The Literacy Initiative, LLC.

541 Tenth Street Suite 258, Atlanta, Georgia 30318

Cover and Interior Design: Buzz Branding, LLC.

Library of Congress Cataloging-in-Publication Data

CIP data is on file with the Library of Congress.

ISBN: 978-0-9889505-4-2

Printed in the U. S. A.

For my father,

Vance Andrew Truss

I am eternally grateful for your love, guidance, encouragement, and inspiration.

Introduction: A Note from Roz

This book is designed as a resource to help you create effective charts that support the informational text and literature standards. The first section, *Why Charts?* explains why charts make a difference in reading classrooms. There is also a detailed list and explanation of the materials that you need to create and display effective charts.

Each subsequent chapter is devoted to a different reading standard. The chapters are labeled to match the exact standard that it represents. For example, chapter one is all about reading standard one; chapter two is all about reading standard two, and so on. This allows you to easily turn directly to the standard that you need.

Once you turn to the chapter that you need, the very first page of the chapter lists the Common Core anchor standard. Anchor standards are the broad, overarching standards that apply to all grade levels. Underneath the anchor standard are the literature and informational text standards broken down by grade level. You can easily find your grade level, highlight your standard, and review the specific language of that standard. The standards are worded exactly as they are on the Common Core State Standards Initiative website, sponsored by the National Governors Association Center for Best Practices (NGA Center) and the Council of Chief State School Officers (CCSSO). You can access this directly at: http://www.corestandards.org.

Each additional page features a different instructional chart specific to the reading standard. Detailed notes are provided to explain how the chart can help readers, how to create your own chart, and any grade-level specifications for that chart.

While there are many different charts included here, the idea is not for you to create each chart! The goal is to give you some ideas to support instruction. These charts can be duplicated exactly as they are pictured here or varied and adapted for your classroom. If you adapt a chart or create an even more dynamic version, reach out to let me know! I am always excited to see and hear what new ideas and creative instructional decisions teachers make. Questions? Need help? Reach out to me online at www.rozlinder.com. Happy teaching!

Dr. Roz

Why Charts?

There are so many benefits to using charts to help make student learning visible. With the new, challenging Common Core reading standards, students need more support than ever to make sense of complex text. Shared visuals are an easy and effective way to help support readers. I find that students have a stronger sense of ownership over the content, use the charts as learning tools more often, and are more engaged and interested.

1. Students will have a shared sense of ownership over the content.

You are creating these charts *with* your students. This is not a situation where you tell them to do something and hope that they do it. This is something that you create with your students through discussion, questioning, and a shared sense of learning. You will notice that students revel in having their writing on a chart or recognizing the sections that they contributed to. When a shared chart falls off the wall, your students will actually rush to pick it up and get it back into place. These shared creations will belong to the entire class.

2. Students will use the charts!

You can easily visit your favorite school supply store to stock up on lots of charts to decorate the walls of your classroom. Those charts may be attractive, but do they really impact instruction? How many times have you seen a student use one of those commercial charts? Five? Ten? Make one chart *with* your students, and watch how many more times they use that chart!

3. Visuals are engaging!

Charts give students a visual reminder of what is expected, how to get there, and ways to troubleshoot. Often, students may not ask for help or admit that they don't remember a strategy. Having a consistent visual reminder is an appealing way to trigger their memories and to keep their attention. Think about the typical fashion magazine. Some of these magazines are 50% advertisements! From a financial standpoint that infuriates me, but I still catch myself gazing at the attractive spreads to see what they are selling. My curiosity is piqued, and I actually keep the image in my head. Creating an attractive visual *with* your students is just one way to tap into that same phenomenon, but for reading.

Different Types of Charts

There are many different types of charts. They can be organized and classified in a dozen (or more) different ways by a dozen (or more) different experts. I like to think about charts as reminders for students. They help students to keep track of their learning and to apply it. Relying on this belief, I classify charts into four key areas:

1. Ritual

2. Toolbox

3. Classification

4. Interactive

Ritual

These types of traditional charts can be found in virtually every K-12 classroom. Ritual charts usually display the basic rules that students should follow. These can include behavior, classroom expectations, or arrival/dismissal procedures. Many of the procedural charts that teachers make for writing and reading workshops often fall into this category as well. Ritual charts are introduced at the beginning of the year or unit, and they rarely change. These charts, while important, are very specific to your own classroom. They will vary based on the norms, beliefs, and programs adopted by your school and district. As a result, *K-2 Chart Sense* does not include this type of chart.

Toolbox

Toolbox charts remind me of a day, not too long ago, when I watched a car mechanic pulling out his red, weathered toolbox to try to diagnose my car. The tattered toolbox seemed to be filled with everything he needed. I watched with curiosity as he lifted my hood, then proceeded to pull out a wide variety of tools. I found myself questioning and wondering what exactly was going on. What was that black thing? Why does he have two of those? What is that pointy thing? Why did he put that tool back in the box?

Toolbox chart example

Readers also rely on a toolbox of strategies and steps that help them make meaning of text. Toolbox charts represent that collection of strategies. Readers certainly aren't fixing a car with these tools, but they are just as powerful. Toolbox charts help students to understand options for what to do when they struggle, get confused, or need help determining what to do next. These types of charts could include steps to follow when working on a specific standard or problem-solving strategies. Toolbox charts are introduced throughout the year. They can help you introduce a unit of study or serve as activators. These charts are also created in response to student performance. If I notice that most of my readers are coming to a roadblock when they encounter new vocabulary, I may develop a chart that helps them understand the concrete steps that they need to follow when they encounter a new word. I often add additional information to these charts throughout the year as students develop new reading skills and tools.

Classification

Classification charts can be used when your students need to understand unique or different characteristics. For example, genre charts that list the features of poems or stories would fit in this category. Classification charts are also useful when students need to compare and contrast.   Teachers can use these to help students keep track of big ideas and distinguish concepts. Students use these charts as visuals that show how two ideas or concepts are different. These can be in the form of lists, Venn diagrams, or other graphics. Classification charts can also be used to develop initial understanding or to redirect a misunderstanding. They can be introduced at any time throughout the year.

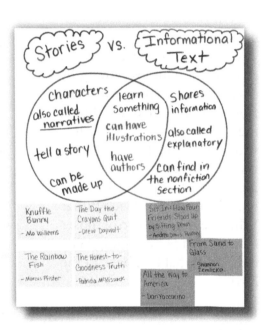

Classification chart example

Interactive

Interactive charts are my absolute favorite. I find that students learn the most from these types of charts. Interactive charts can be static or reusable.

Students generate the information, and it is specific to a particular text. For example, if I teach my students to retell a story, we would also create a chart to go along with it. This chart would be a summary (or portion of a summary) that we would write as a class. This collaborative process results in meaningful charts that differ from year to year. Not only are these charts created *with the students,* but they also include an active think-aloud modeling session. Think-aloud modeling means that as you write, you stop to question, wonder, and let students have a peek into your cognitive process. Interactive charts usually remain in a prominent place, and they serve as exemplars.

Sticky notes work hand-in-hand with this type of chart. For example, as students read books and talk about their reading, they can use sticky notes to record their ideas and thoughts. Interactive charts are great spaces to share and post these ideas. The sticky notes can also be removed or repositioned depending on the book or new standard that your class is focusing on.

Please keep in mind that each of these different chart categories are not rigid boxes that must remain separate. There will be overlap, and some charts could belong in more than one category. The category is not the most important thing here; the teaching is.

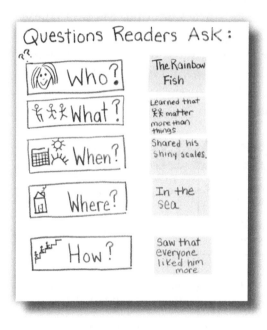

Interactive chart example

Materials to Create Great Charts

It is not necessary to be an artist or to spend tons of money to create effective charts for your readers. There are some basic tools that you will want to have on hand to make charts easily.

Chart Paper

There are many different brands and styles of chart paper. There are types that have adhesive on the back and can be stuck right onto the wall. These work well, but they will eventually lose their adhesive quality and possibly fall down. This process will happen even faster if you move your charts around a lot. The easy solution is to add tape. *But…if I have to add tape, then I might as well use regular chart paper, right?* Well, there are pros and cons to all types of chart paper. Let's take a look:

Paper Type	Benefits	Disadvantages
Adhesive-Back Chart Paper	You can quickly attach these to any wall in seconds. These are readily available in most office supply stores.	These may eventually fall down without the addition of more tape. This is the most expensive choice.
Non-Adhesive Chart Paper	Most school and office supply stores carry this paper. This is the most inexpensive choice.	You must use tape or magnets to display this type of chart.
Half-Sized Chart Paper	These are great for quick charts that don't require a full-size sheet.	You may still need to purchase full-size paper for larger charts.
Non-Adhesive Colored Chart Paper	These bright charts are the most attractive of all the options.	A limited number of stores carry this paper. This is more expensive than plain white chart paper.

Chart paper comes in a variety of sizes and colors. One of the largest sizes of chart paper is 25"x30". This size chart comes in yellow or white. You can choose lined, blank, or grid-lined for the surfaces. This size chart paper is used for most of the charts in this book. If you are interested in colored chart paper, Pacon® sells spiral bound chart paper that is about this same size (24"x32") and comes in assorted pastel colors. For brighter colors, consider Top Notch Teacher Products' 24"x32" neon chart paper. Also spiral bound, these tablets contain eye-catching deep oranges, greens, pinks, and blues. The second largest size, 20"x23", is commonly associated with easel pads. This size comes unlined, with primary lines, and blank. Finally, there are small, colored paper chart tablets that are about half the size of the larger size chart paper. At 24"x16", these charts take up less space and work well for charts that contain small amounts of information.

Sticky Notes

Sticky notes are essential when creating reusable charts. They can easily be filled out in advance and repositioned as necessary. In order to maximize this flexibility, I try to keep a wide variety on hand. Post-it® brand notes are readily available in many shapes, sizes, and colors. One of my favorites is the large 8"x6" size. This size sticky note is used a lot for the large headings and for many of the interactive charts. The small 4"x4" sticky notes are very common, but often too small to fit

Sticky notes come in a wide variety of sizes and colors.

much text on. 6"x4" sticky notes are larger and work well when you need students to write information for charts. Both of these sizes tend to cost more, but they really help your charts stand out and provide more space to write on.

A cheaper alternative to emulate the effect of the oversized sticky note is to grab a pack of colored paper and tape. You can cut the paper into any shape or size, then use a small amount of tape to stick the note onto your chart. Another cost-cutting alternative is to buy the store-brand sticky notes at discount or dollar stores.

Thin-Tip Markers

I like to have thin, student-friendly markers on hand. Many brands categorize these types of markers as fine-tip or fine-point markers. These markers work best for your students to use when they need to write on the charts or add information. These thin markers also come in handy when you need to illustrate something more elaborate or draw a simple detail. Crayola®, Rose Art®, and Sharpie® all sell great thin-tip markers. I have even found several office supply store brands to work just as well.

Wide-Tip Markers

I use wide-tip markers most frequently when writing on charts. I have tried many different brands, shapes, and sizes. This choice really comes down to personal preference. For a long time, I relied only on the scented Mr. Sketch® markers. In the past few years I have also discovered the wide-tip Sharpie® brand markers. Both brands are excellent choices for making charts. Be careful to avoid any markers that are labeled as "poster markers." These tend to be much too big for charts, and they also bleed through chart paper.

Sentence Strips

Sentence strips are long pieces of sturdy paper, resembling cardstock. One side has a guideline rule, while the other has a single line. You can find sentence strips in white, beige, rainbow, and pastel colors at school supply stores and big-box retailers. They only cost a few dollars and one pack goes a long way.

In the nineties, when I first started creating charts with my students, I never even thought about adding sentence strips to a chart. Why would I do that? Couldn't I just write the same information on the actual chart or on a sticky note? Eventually, I found that sentence strips were surprisingly useful when making charts. They are larger than most sticky notes and much more durable. They also come in handy when students need to record more than just a few words on a chart. There are times when you will need to add book titles, long phrases, or even lengthy passages of text to a chart. Sentence strips provide the extra space necessary to do this.

Scissors

You want to keep a pair of reliable scissors on hand. There will be times when you will need them to cut your sticky notes and sentence strips into various shapes and sizes. Consider using craft scissors with different types of edges to add a decorative effect. These come in zig-zag, scallop, ripple, and curved shapes. Typically sold in sets of six or twelve, these scissors are available at most craft stores and big box retailers. Popular brands include Fiskars® and X-Acto®. Make sure that you have a few extra pairs on hand for student use as well.

Adhesive

Masking tape is a useful resource to keep on hand. You will need this to hold charts up and attach paper to the charts. I prefer this type of tape because it can easily be removed when you need to reposition different elements of your chart. If you are a fan of clear or double-sided tape, be certain that what you are taping down does not need to be manipulated by your students often. The last thing you want to do is rip a hole in one of your charts.

Space for Charts

Every classroom is arranged differently, and school districts have varied rules about how wall space can be used. Optimally, you will have lots of blank walls and the ability to put as much (or as little) on the walls as you choose. In reality, this is rarely the case. It is usually necessary to explore alternative options for displaying your charts. If your students cannot see the charts, they can't use them. Here are some of the ways I display my charts.

The Clothesline

I first started using the clothesline method when I was a fourth-grade teacher. I bought an actual clothesline at a big-box retailer, two nails, and plastic clothespins. I asked our wonderful custodian if he would place the two nails in opposite corners of my room. We hung a clothesline that spanned the length of my classroom. I learned a few valuable lessons that year. When you hang such a long clothesline diagonally, only half of the class can see any particular chart at the same time. I also learned that chart paper doesn't like to stay attached to a clothesline without reinforcement. One chart actually took four or five plastic clothespins to stay in place. Also, this meant that our entire class was always drowning under a sea of charts.

The next year I reworked my whole clothesline idea. I had to admit that I'd grown overly attached to my charts, and just wanted my handiwork visible at all times! That was the wrong approach; I had to let it go. This time I hung the clothesline flat against one wall. I learned that I did not need every chart hanging up at the same time. Only charts that students are actively using need to be displayed in a classroom.

Magnets

One simple way to display your charts is to hang them on a chalkboard or a whiteboard using magnets. Two or three magnets will easily hold up most charts. The use of magnets gives you the flexibility to post and remove your charts as needed. This also allows metal file cabinets or any other metal surfaces in your classroom to become display areas.

Hangers

Skirt or pants hangers work well to display charts. You should be able to inexpensively pick up a few at the local dollar store. When buying clothing from any retailer, ask the cashier if you can keep your hangers. You can even ask for some of the extra hangers that are almost always in a big box under the cash register. I have walked out of stores with over thirty pants hangers. It doesn't hurt to ask!

A chart hung from a pants hanger

Once you have your hangers, you can use them to easily hang any non-laminated charts. Laminated charts tend to be slippery and will slide out of the clips. You can store your charts by hanging them out of the way on doors or cabinets until you need them. You can also use a garment stand to hold the hangers. I like this idea because your students can go over and access any chart that they need, even after you retire it from the wall. If you live close to an IKEA, consider purchasing a *Rigga* or a *Mulig* clothing stand. Both stands cost around ten dollars apiece and can even be ordered online at www.ikea.com.

Hidden Gems

Don't overlook the obvious. A chart can be displayed in many different places. If you have fabric curtains covering a bookcase, grab two safety pins and attach your chart to the front of the curtain. Depending on how your room is organized, the marker or chalk holder at the base of your chalkboard or whiteboard is a perfect space to hang several charts. Do you have large classroom cabinets? The doors and sides of those cabinets could be great landing spots for charts. Check out your classroom windows, the front of your desk, the bottom of a mounted television, or even the extra space above your chalkboard. Think about places that normally go untouched. Be creative and look for hidden gems!

Chapter 1

Ask and Answer Questions

Common Core Reading Anchor Standard 1:
Read closely to determine what the text says explicitly and make logical inferences from it; cite specific textual evidence when writing or speaking to support conclusions drawn from the text.

	Literary Text	**Informational Text**
K	With prompting and support, ask and answer questions about details in a text.	With prompting and support, ask and answer questions about key details in a text.
1	Ask and answer questions about key details in a text.	Ask and answer questions about key details in a text.
2	Ask and answer such questions as who, what, where, when, why, and how to demonstrate understanding of key details in a text.	Ask and answer such questions as who, what, where, when, why, and how to demonstrate understanding of key details in a text.

Ask and Answer

This is one of those charts that I hesitated to include; the crooked line and sloppy letters almost caused this chart to end up in the trash bin. After a bit of thought, I realized that this type of chart is exactly what needed to be in this book. Charts aren't perfect; teachers aren't artists. The point is to make learning visible for kids. So this chart, flaws and all, made its way into the book. This chart works for both literature and informational text. Students are expected to ask and answer questions about the books that they read. This easy-to-make chart helps to make these questions visible.

Introducing This Chart:

After reading a book about matter out loud, I asked students to pretend that they were teachers. *What questions could we ask other students who had read this book?* This guiding question helped us to fill in the right side of this chart. We even answered our own questions in the parentheses. Afterwards, I asked students what they still wanted to know. *What questions were unanswered?* This guiding question helped us to complete the left side of the chart.

Teaching Ideas:

1. Place empty laminated charts in centers and ask students to draw pictures that represent what they want to ask or can answer about a text. Students can place their pictures on the chart and explain what questions they represent. While I rarely laminate charts, I do suggest lamination for interactive charts that will be independently handled by students in centers.

2. This is a great chart for science and social studies. Use this in place of KWL charts to discuss content-area reading.

3. Fill in the answer section on your own and call on students to generate responses to these questions as a quick formative assessment.

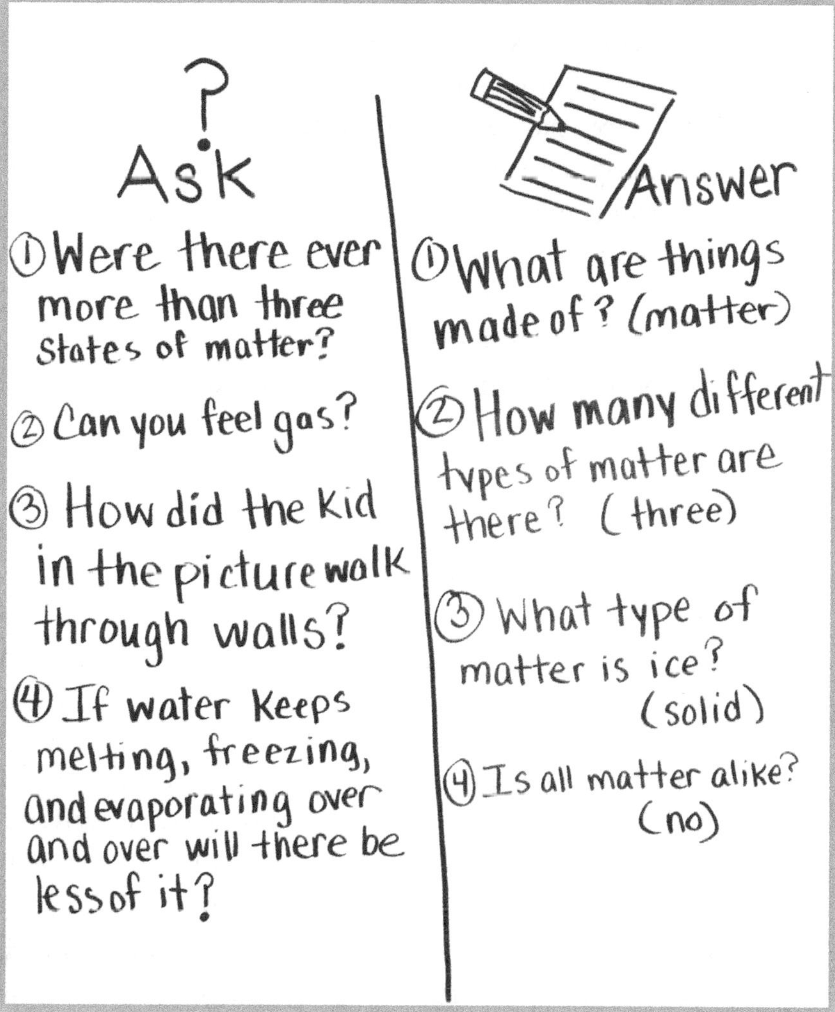

Ask

① Were there ever more than three states of matter?

② Can you feel gas?

③ How did the kid in the picture walk through walls?

④ If water keeps melting, freezing, and evaporating over and over will there be less of it?

Answer

① What are things made of? (matter)

② How many different types of matter are there? (three)

③ What type of matter is ice? (solid)

④ Is all matter alike? (no)

Figure 1.1 *Ask and Answer* chart

Beginning, Middle, and End

This chart was created with first graders. Before I read *Madeline* by Ludwig Bemelmans, I asked students to think about what parts of the text they would share to retell this story to a parent. After reading the text, I led a brief discussion about the best parts of the book. I like to do this to give students who may not fully understand the text a chance to hear the ideas of others and have a moment to connect the ideas and events. After our discussion, students shared which events happened in the beginning, middle, and end of the text. Each of these ideas were added to the chart.

Variations:

- Consider writing the major events on index cards or sentence strips. Ask students to work in groups to place them in time-sequence order. When students are working at their desks, you may want to skip asking students to classify with the terms *beginning, middle,* and *end.* It can be a very fuzzy area determining if an event falls in the middle or the beginning without teacher guidance. A strong case can often be made for either. Asking students to place events in time-sequence order targets the standard just as effectively.

- If you use picture rubrics in your classroom, consider replacing the flower pot pictures with the same type of images that you use on your rubrics. I have seen houses, sunrises, and caterpillars/ butterflies used.

- Use images to represent the different parts of the story instead of sentences. This is particularly effective if you have a large number of nonreaders in your classroom.

 **Beginning**

- Old house in Paris

- We meet 12 good girls

- The youngest is Madeline.

 Middle

- Madeline gets sick

- Madeline leaves with the doctor.

- She had to get surgery.

 End

- Miss Clavel and the girls go to visit Madeline.

- Madeline has lots of toys, candy, and a big dollhouse.

- Everyone of the girls want to get the same surgery, too.

Figure 1.2 *Beginning, Middle, and End chart*

Big Events

This chart works well with any grade level, but due to the amount of written text, it is more appropriate for first and second grade. In addition to working with multiple grade levels, this chart can also be created to meet the rigor of the informational text or literature standard.

Introducing This Chart:

This fun chart was created after reading *The True Story of the Three Little Pigs* by Jon Scieszka. We simply discussed the book and briefly explored the idea of an "unreliable narrator." Students were intrigued by this concept. We also talked about times when the students may have told stories and been unreliable narrators themselves. After our discussion, I drew the columns and wrote the headings. I called on students to share ideas for the big events. I wrote these on large 8"x6" sticky notes and added them to the chart. After each one, I stopped and thought out loud, using "*I wonder…*" as my thinking stem. Then, I asked students what they wondered about this event. Finally, I asked students what they learned from this event. *What did this answer or clear up?* This information was added to the right column.

Teaching Ideas:

1. When you ask students for ideas there will be multiple responses. Due to space limitations and to accommodate the numerous responses, consider migrating this chart to a wall or whiteboard to access more space.

2. When you first introduce this standard, try to select a book that is engaging and/or connects to your readers. While students will need to ask and answer questions about all texts (engaging or not), it really helps them to grasp the concept when it is introduced through a topic or story that they enjoy or can relate to.

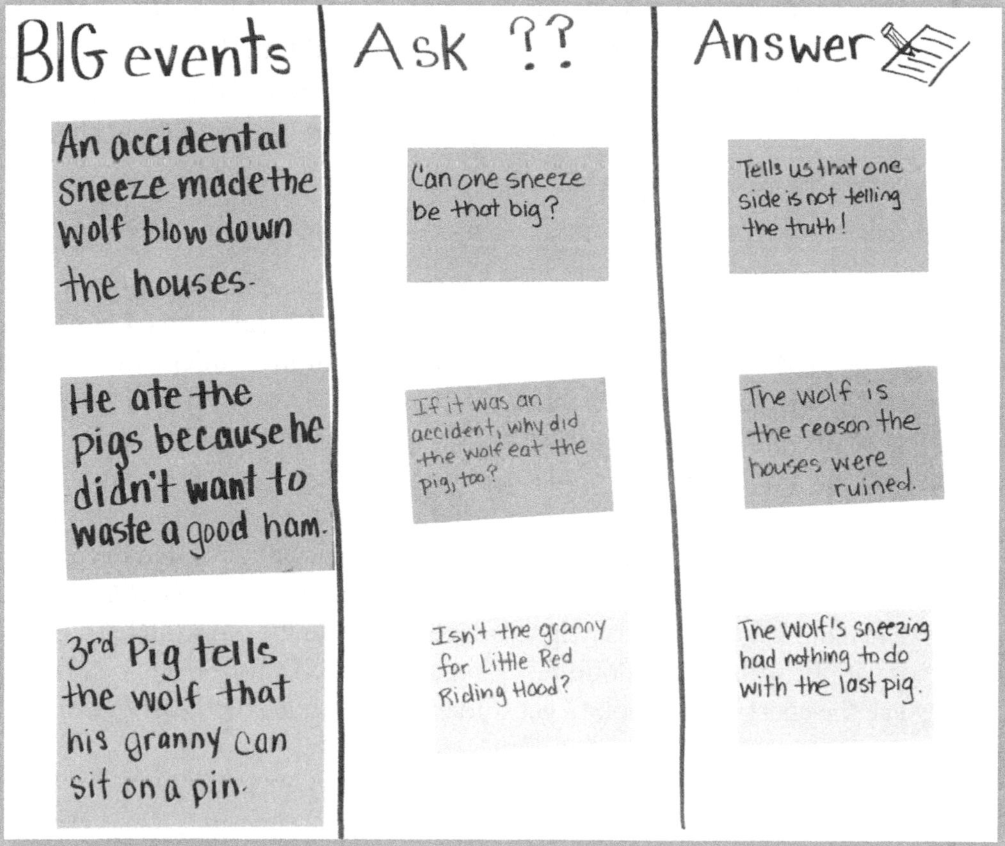

BIG events	Ask ??	Answer ✎
An accidental sneeze made the wolf blow down the houses.	Can one sneeze be that big?	Tells us that one side is not telling the truth!
He ate the pigs because he didn't want to waste a good ham.	If it was an accident, why did the wolf eat the pig, too?	The wolf is the reason the houses were ruined.
3rd Pig tells the wolf that his granny can sit on a pin.	Isn't the granny for Little Red Riding Hood?	The Wolf's sneezing had nothing to do with the last pig.

Figure 1.3 *Big Events* chart

High Five!

This chart is a great visual for helping students think about the 5Ws embedded within a text. Interactive and fun, this chart can easily work with both literature and informational text. We worked on the literature standard when making this chart.

Creating This Chart:

Drawing a giant hand is always a challenge for me. No matter how many times I do it, the result is a bit strange looking. To combat this, I create the large hand in advance, but write the labels with my students. I find that each term needs to be explicitly discussed with young readers. To help students make sense of the questions, I ask students to think of something that has just happened in our classroom. Perhaps someone told a funny joke, or a student brought in a pet to show the class, or maybe I did something that was memorable. I ask students to think of that event. As I add the questions to each finger, I ask *who was involved, what happened, when did it happen?* This helps students to situate the question before they try it out with a read-aloud text. You can even do this the day before you use the chart with a book to get students comfortable with the questions.

Teaching Ideas:

- Consider creating this chart by rereading a class favorite. For this chart, we reread *Miss Nelson is Missing* by Harry Allard. Next, we responded to each question together, pausing to think aloud and interact.

- After this has been introduced, consider asking students to pick one finger and tell you something about the book that you have just read. Make it a fun game and enjoyable!

- Draw a hand on paper and photocopy it. Place multiple copies of the handout in a literacy station or a center for students to use with their independent reading.

- Students can even trace their own hands at the desks to use when they read a text independently.

Figure 1.4 *High Five!* chart

Questions Readers Ask

This chart is a great way to match basic comprehension questions to visual images. This connection is critical for new readers who are still making sense of print. A student may not recognize all of the words, but still be able to associate the image of the girl with *Who?*, or the calendar and sunrise with *When?*. Create images that your students can connect to. Notice that I did not include *Why?* on the chart. As teachers, we are used to asking the 5Ws and H questions collectively. I have finally realized that every question is not needed for every text. Choose the questions that you want to focus on. To see other question combinations, view the *High Five!* or *Readers Wonder* anchor charts.

Creating This Chart:

I created this chart from start to finish with students. After we read and discussed *The Rainbow Fish* by Marc Pfister (a great book that you can purchase used on Amazon for about a penny), we read each question and talked about what the question really asked us. Then, I organized students into small groups to discuss the answer to each question. Afterwards, I called on students and we decided on the best answer to place on the chart.

Be Prepared!

There are so many different ways to explain a story that there will be numerous ideas for each question that are not necessarily wrong, but focus on different angles and aspects of a book. To illustrate this, think about the story of Cinderella. The *where* could be the ball or her home. The *what* could be to get away from her stepsisters, to marry the prince, or to make it home before midnight. Be prepared for this! I spent a lot of time telling groups that they had very good answers, but that, for the class chart, we were going to focus on a different event. In retrospect, I could have added all of the choices to the chart.

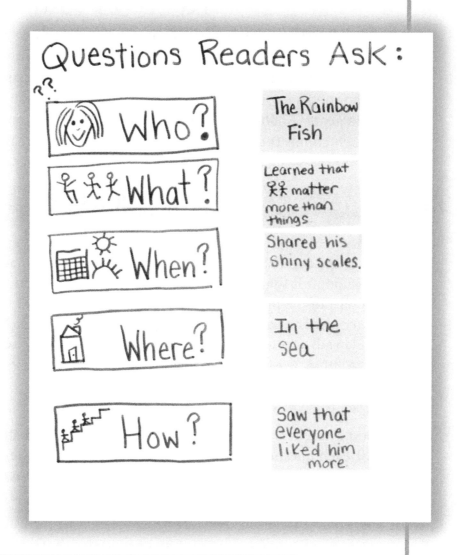

Questions Readers Ask:

Who?		The Rainbow Fish
What?		Learned that 웃웃 matter more than things
When?		Shared his shiny scales.
Where?		In the sea
How?		Saw that everyone liked him more

Figure 1.5 *Questions Readers Ask* chart

Readers Wonder

This chart is about connecting the questions to an image. The types of images that you choose to draw can and should vary to relate to your students. In this first grade class, we had just finished a lesson on action words (verbs). We had spent a lot of time *jumping, hopping, singing,* and *running.* The *–ing* ending was very much connected to action for these students. Create images that connect specifically with your students to make the concept stick!

Creating This Chart:

Try to create this entire chart *with* your students. As tempting as it is to make this chart more attractive by drawing it in advance, the whole point is that the chart is a shared creation. Students need to be a part of the process and invested in the content. If this terrifies you, consider creating the questions or images on large 8"x6" sticky notes in advance and adding them to the chart during the discussion with your students.

Variations:

- Some teachers use smaller 24"x16" charts and create one chart for each question. Underneath each question, teachers write real examples. For example, student names, book characters, people from the school, and historical figures are placed under the *Who?* question.

- Use these charts as a connection to writing. Ask students to use these questions when creating their own narratives.

- When you read aloud, call on students to respond to each of the questions. Record the different responses on sticky notes and build a bank of people, places, and settings that students have read about throughout the school year.

Figure 1.6 *Readers Wonder* chart

Chapter 2

Main Topics and Messages

Common Core Reading Anchor Standard 2:
Determine central ideas or themes of a text and analyze their development; summarize the key supporting details and ideas.

	Literary Text	Informational Text
K	With prompting and support, retell familiar stories, including key details.	With prompting and support, identify the main topic and retell key details of a text.
1	Retell stories, including key details, and demonstrating understanding of their central message or lesson.	Identify the main topic, and retell key details in a text.
2	Recount stories, including fables and folktales from diverse cultures, and determine their central message, lesson or moral.	Identify the main topic of a multiparagraph text as well as the focus of specific paragraphs within the text.

Lessons From Books

I enjoy teaching students about lessons, morals, and messages. This standard is meaningful because there is no one correct answer. Readers can take away different messages from the same book. You will be surprised at the wide variety of ideas! My own daughter told me that the lesson from "Little Red Riding Hood" was to mind your own business and don't be a snoop. I would not have said it that way, but she was right! Keep this in mind when working on this standard. It is not that students should see the world as you do; it is about them thinking critically and justifying the messages that they take away from different stories.

Introducing This Chart:

1. I gathered three different books that I felt were reflective of three different lessons. I chose *The Little Engine that Could, A Bad Case of the Stripes*, and *Eli's Lie-o-Meter*. In one sitting, I read each book out loud.

2. Then, I added each of the three preselected messages to the chart and asked students if they thought that a reader could learn any of these messages from these books. At this point, we went back into the books. We turned to different pages and reread sections as students attempted to convince me (and each other) that different messages were inherent in the books.

3. Finally, we added the name of each book next to one of the different messages.

4. As we read more books, the list continued to grow. This chart represents several weeks.

Teaching Ideas:

• Type each message in a large font. Print out all of the messages horizontally on colored paper and tape these to a cabinet or wall in your classroom. Each time you read a book, photocopy the book cover at 35% and place it under the message. By the end of the year, you will have a great visual trail of books read, organized by message.

• Focus on one or two messages for the month or semester. Write each of these messages on a chart of their own. Add book names throughout the year and hang above or below your chalkboard for student reference.

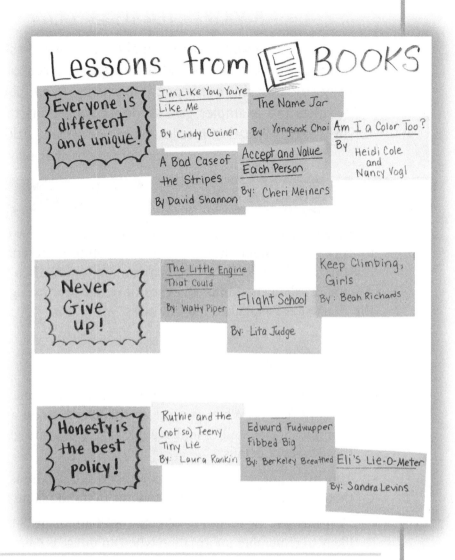

Lessons from BOOKS

Everyone is different and unique!

I'm Like You, You're Like Me
By Cindy Gainer

The Name Jar
By: Yangsook Choi

Am I a Color Too?
By Heidi Cole and Nancy Vogl

A Bad Case of the Stripes
By David Shannon

Accept and Value Each Person
By: Cheri Meiners

Never Give Up!

The Little Engine That Could
By: Watty Piper

Flight School
By: Lita Judge

Keep Climbing, Girls
By: Beah Richards

Honesty is the best policy!

Ruthie and the (not so) Teeny Tiny Lie
By: Laura Rankin

Edward Fudwupper Fibbed Big
By: Berkeley Breathed

Eli's Lie-O-Meter
By: Sandra Levins

Figure 2.1 *Lessons from Books* chart

Main Topics are Heavy

The second grade informational text standard asks students to recognize main topics and the supporting reasons/details. For primary students, this concept can be fuzzy. *What does a detail look like?* Lists and examples give students something tangible to look for in a text. Instead of just looking for reasons, students can look for sentences that play specific roles.

Creating This Chart:

This basic chart was created with second graders. I drew (or attempted to draw) a stick figure lifting a heavy barbell to represent the role that reasons and details play in supporting main topics. Then I simply led a discussion about the different types of details, recording each one on the chart after I explained it to the class.

Teaching Ideas:

- Select informational text excerpts that include examples of the different types of details. When you create this chart, share and discuss one example. Social studies and science text books are great sources for these types of details.

- This list is not static; add additional types of details as you encounter them in text. Encourage your students to do the same thing.

- Consider pairing each type of detail with an image. Students are more likely to remember information when an image is paired with text.

- Use this chart with your daily reading. When reading any informational text, stop and ask what "job" a sentence has. *How does the sentence support the main topic?*

- Remember that entire passages can have a main topic as well as individual paragraphs. This concept applies to both. Make sure that students recognize this as well.

Main Topics are heavy!

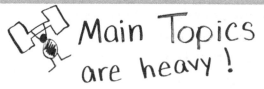

What details hold them up?

- describing words (descriptions)
- comparisons
- what the topic does
- why the topic is important
- what the topic is just like
- where the topic is located
- how the topic works
- how the topic grows or changes

Figure 2.2 *Main Topics are Heavy* chart

Main Topics

This simple puzzle chart was used to introduce students to four questions that they can consider when looking for details in an informational text passage. "It" refers to the main topic of a passage. For example, if students are reading about the solar system and want to locate details, they can easily look for sentences that answer each of the questions posted on the chart. These questions will help guide students to supporting details in a text. These specific four questions are clearly not the only choices for this task, but suggested starting points. Some teachers also change the pronouns on this chart. For example, when students read about a person and use this chart, the word "it" might be replaced with "him" or "her." Some teachers actually replace the word "it" with "it/him/her" on the chart instead. This is a personal preference based on your students and teaching style.

Variations:

1. Create this chart as you read an informational text with your students. Be intentional and select a text that features clear, easy-to-find responses to each question. Call on students to answer each one as you read aloud.

2. Consider adding sticky notes to the chart that feature common responses to these questions. This will give students ideas of what types of sentences or words might be included in a response. For example, under *What does it look like?*, you might add words like *tall, large, very small, yellow, blue,* etc. These references can come in handy for students as they navigate text and make meaning.

3. Add images next to each question to help students remember what types of things to look for. This is a fun and simple addition that can help each question resonate with students.

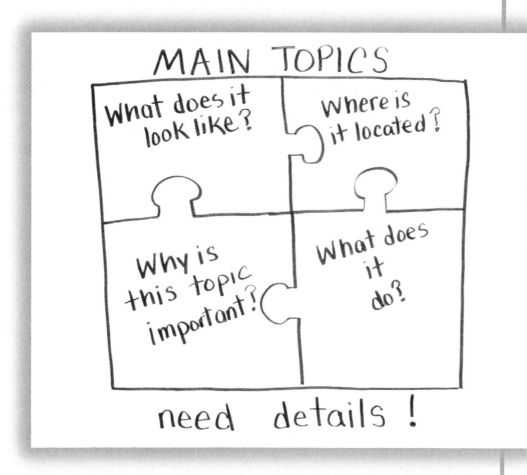

Figure 2.3 *Main Topics* chart

Morals and Lessons

Themes, lessons, morals, and messages are integral parts of this standard in every grade level from elementary through high school. Despite the prevalence, these concepts are challenging to explain and teach. The goal of this chart is to make these terms less abstract and offer students concrete examples of ideas that constitute lessons and messages. Each grade level standard is written to include slightly different terminology, so be sure to include the words that fit for your grade level.

Terminology:

Students in upper elementary begin to use the term *theme*. Primary students use the terms: *message, lesson,* or *moral*. Many teachers confuse these with *topics*. I often see lists of messages that include terms such as *honesty* or *friendship*. These are topics rather than messages. For example, honesty can be the topic of a book; honesty cannot be a lesson. A lesson should be some type of declarative statement. So instead of honesty, the lesson might be that *honesty is the best policy*. Think of a clear directive that anyone could follow or apply to their day-to-day actions.

Teaching Ideas:

1. Consider introducing one message/lesson at a time. Decide on the message that you want to introduce to your students first. After you identify the message, select short picture books that reflect that lesson. Read the books first, then share the lesson. Ask students to explain how each book communicates a lesson. If students disagree, encourage them to share why and/or offer a different lesson. Throughout the year, build the list by adding new lessons to the chart.

2. Ask students to share times from their own lives where they learned a similar lesson.

3. Expand the discussion beyond books to include movies, television shows, songs, and poems. Shel Silverstein's *Where the Sidewalk Ends* offers a wide variety of poems that include messages and lessons.

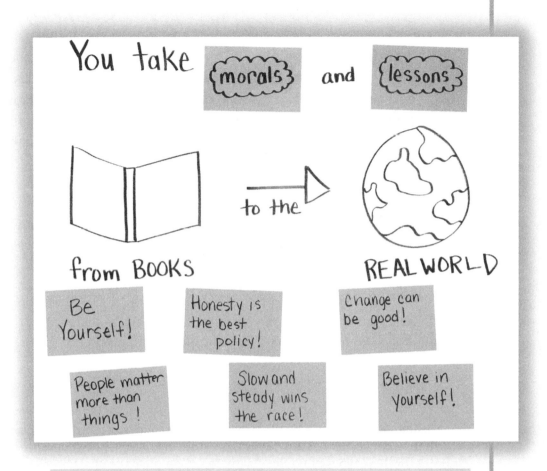

Figure 2.4 *Morals and Lessons* chart

Retell Familiar Stories

This fun chart is a simple variation of the well-known *Somebody Wanted Something* chart (I'm unsure who first developed that). I adapted this chart to make it more of a cloze activity, yet reusable and interactive. The empty boxes provide spaces where students can add information from different stories.

Creating This Chart:

I created this chart with students by drawing the five boxes and then adding the title. Before I wrote the words, I told students that these five little boxes were going to give them a great shortcut to retell stories. Then, I added the four words next to the boxes. Next, we worked together, as a class, to decide what information to add to each box. You can also include punctuation to make the chart read like a set of sentences, or leave it off. I chose to create this chart without punctuation.

Variations:

1. Consider watching a video clip or short animated version of a book. Often media seems less threatening to students, and it is a great entry point for these types of retelling activities. Complete the chart based on this alternative version.

2. Laminate this chart and reuse it after each read-aloud story. This can easily become a predictable step during storytelling time.

3. Place this chart, tape, and index cards in a literacy center or station. Ask students to complete the chart based on the independent books that they read.

4. Create a smaller version of this chart, or type it up as a handout. Ask students to complete the chart when they listen to books on tape or view read-alouds. A great YouTube site with hundreds of read-alouds is: https://www.youtube.com/user/StoryTimeMomShy/videos.

Figure 2.5 *Retell Familiar Stories* chart

Steps to Find Details

This chart was completed with second grade students and is basically a set of "clues" that help students identify details in informational text. This list is not exhaustive and can easily be altered to meet your class's needs.

Introducing This Chart:

1. When I introduced this chart, I displayed a short informational text passage on the whiteboard from www.readworks.org. This website has searchable lexiled passages that are appropriate for K-2 students.

2. After I read the passage aloud, I asked students if they saw any descriptions, places, examples, reasons, or numbers while I created the first half of the chart. It was helpful to have the passage displayed on the whiteboard and the chart on an easel right next to it. Students can easily search the passage and reference the chart.

3. After we completed the first half of the chart, I led a discussion about the three questions under step two and added each one to the chart.

Teaching Ideas:

- Project a text onto the whiteboard or overhead. Color-code the sentences based on what they "do." For example, descriptions could be red, numbers could be green, and so on. Treat this like a scavenger hunt, challenging students to identify what specific lines of text do.

- Link this chart to writing. When students write informational text, ask them to explicitly include and identify the descriptions, places, examples, reasons, or numbers in their own texts.

- Create a signal that students can use when they encounter the different types of details in a text. I have used a bell, hand signals, and rulers. It is fun for students to run over and ring a bell during independent reading to signal that they have noticed a specific type of detail in a book that they are reading.

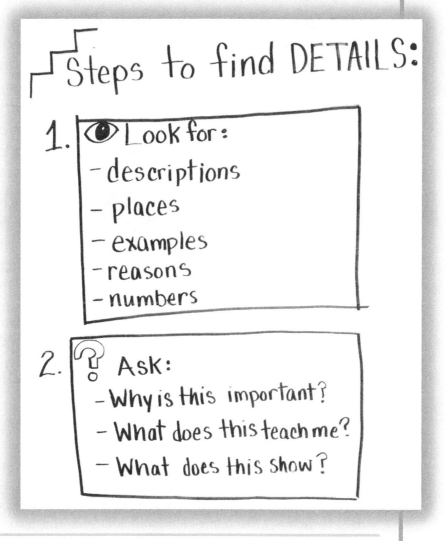

Steps to find DETAILS:

1. 👁 Look for:
   - descriptions
   - places
   - examples
   - reasons
   - numbers

2. ❓ Ask:
   - Why is this important?
   - What does this teach me?
   - What does this show?

Figure 2.6 *Steps to Find Details* chart

We Can Retell Familiar Stories!

This chart focuses on the kindergarten literature standard that asks students to retell familiar stories. This can be challenging for students who are just learning to read and write. To make this task more accessible for all students, I begin the year asking students to use images to retell stories. Students can then illustrate the story and focus on time sequence. Limiting the number of pictures to 3-5 also encourages students to really think about which events are essential to retell the story.

Introducing This Chart:

1. I created this chart by reading Patricia Seibert's *The Three Little Pigs* aloud. I deliberately selected a familiar text to adhere to the language and requirements of this standard.

2. After reading, I drew the three boxes and added the sticky note. I asked students to think about the three biggest, most important parts of the book. Then, I asked students to share their ideas with a neighbor.

3. Next, we shared our ideas as a whole group and actually voted on what image would go in each box. After reaching a consensus, I drew each picture on the chart.

4. After the chart was complete, I called on different students to "read" the chart aloud to retell the story.

Teaching Ideas:

- An alternative to using labels such as beginning, middle, and end is to use characters, setting, problem, and solution. This also connects well with standard seven.

- Create a smaller template for students to use while retelling their own stories. Photocopy several blank templates and keep them in an accessible area for independent reading. Post completed charts around the room.

- Designate a specific day or time as Retelling Day. Students can come to the front or sit in the author's chair to retell a story that they have read.

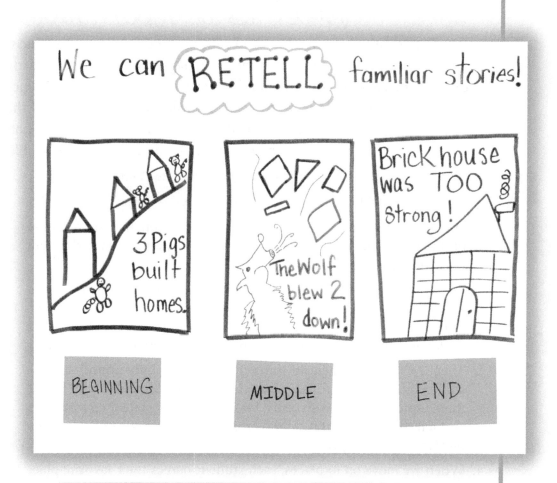

Figure 2.7 *We Can Retell Familiar Stories!* chart

What is a Main Topic?

The terminology used in the reading standards is new to most students. Due to the shifting language used in the standards, explicit instruction with terminology is critical. This chart outlines common types of main topics. You will notice that each of the sticky notes pairs an image with the text. It is a smart idea to pair images with words as often as possible.

Teaching With This Chart:

1. When I create this chart, I only write the question and the response on the chart. Then, I explain that books can be about many different types of main topics.

2. Next, I ask students to stand up. I call out individual names and repeat that each student could be a main topic of an informational text. Finally, I ask all of my main topics to take a seat, while I add my first sticky note that says that a main topic can be a person or an animal.

3. Then, I ask each student to think of an animal. I go around and ask students to share, explaining that each of these animals could be the main topic of a book. For events, I ask everyone to state their birthdays and tell them that those could be main topics. *Wouldn't a book about our birthdays be a great story?*

4. When we move on to places, each student names their favorite place in the school. Sometimes we get up and travel to these places. This results in a fun trip around the school, all the while reinforcing the concept of main topics.

5. For things that work, I pull up Google on the whiteboard and type in "machines." The image section for this search term yields pictures of everything from robots to dump trucks. Students call out the names of the machines and I explain that each of these could be a main topic.

6. While these activities seem like they take up a lot of time, the payoff is unrivaled. Students will have concrete images of different things that can serve as main topics.

What is a MAIN topic?

Sometimes it's a person or animal.

Sometimes it's a place.

Sometimes it's an event.

Sometimes it's a thing that works.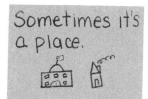

What the text is all about!

Figure 2.8 *What is a Main Topic?* chart

Chapter 3

Characters and Connections

Common Core Reading Anchor Standard 3:
Analyze how and why individuals, events, and ideas develop and interact over the course of a text.

	Literary Text	**Informational Text**
K	With prompting and support, identify characters, settings, and major events in a story.	With prompting and support, describe the connection between two individuals, events, ideas, or pieces of information in a text.
1	Describe characters, settings, and major events in a story, using key details.	Describe the connection between two individuals, events, ideas, or pieces of information in a text.
2	Describe how characters in a story respond to major events and challenges.	Describe the connection between a series of historical events, scientific ideas or concepts, or steps in technical procedures in a text.

Big Challenge

This chart is aligned to the second grade literature standard. It can be used with any grade level, but the level of rigor is most appropriate for second graders. Students use this to explore multiple characters' actions and responses to major challenges in the story.

Teaching Ideas:

- Select a book that features multiple characters. We read *The Monsters' Monster* by Patrick McDonnell. If you want to focus on a singular character, consider using the *Challenge or Event* chart in this chapter.

- While I didn't do this for this chart, a thin marker is useful for the *What did they do to fix up the challenge?* section. I could barely fit the lengthy responses that students gave and had to use abbreviations and rephrase a lot of students' responses. To avoid that, have a thin- or fine-tipped marker on hand.

Being Interactive:

1. I used sticky notes so that we could switch out the different challenges. This is important because books are rarely as linear as we teach them. There are multiple challenges that characters face. The major or big challenge could vary quite a bit and is, at times, subjective. Using removable sticky notes gives you the flexibility to consider multiple ideas.

2. The sticky notes also make this chart reusable. Simply pull off the sticky notes and create this entire chart with another book. Consider retiring the chart to a literacy center or station where students can recreate the chart based on small group readings.

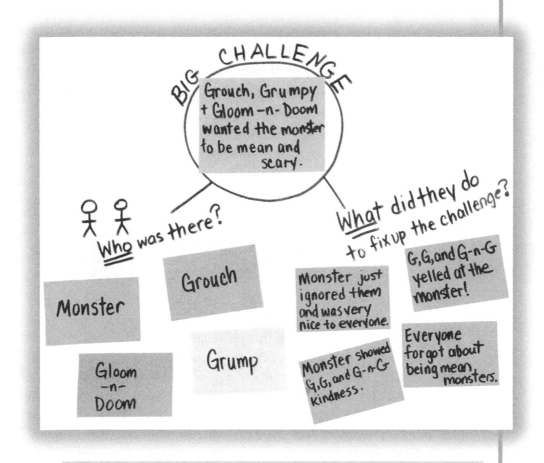

Figure 3.1 *Big Challenge* chart

Challenge or Event

This interactive chart, aligned to the literature standard, was created with second graders. The top portion helps students to think about the characters in a text and their challenges. The last column is for students to consider how characters respond to these challenges.

Creating This Chart:

1. I created this chart from start to finish with the students.

2. To make this chart reusable, I wrote each challenge or event on removable 8"x6" sticky notes.

3. The remaining text is written on 6"x4" sticky notes.

Introducing This Chart:

1. I introduced this chart over two days. On the first day, I asked students to think about times when they were afraid, confused, or proud. As they shared, I drew the top part of this chart and matched the events and actions in their story to each of the three chart headings. For example, when a student began a story by saying, "when I was five . . ." I would draw the stick figure and point out that this story was about a person in our class. As the student continued, I added the sticky note for the event and directly referenced the events that the student described. Finally, when the student told how he or she responded, I referenced that on the chart as well. I repeated this with about five students before I moved on to a book.

2. I decided to reread two books that the students were already familiar with: *A Bad Case of the Stripes* by David Shannon and *The Boy Who Cried Ninja* by Alex Latimer.

3. Next, we talked about each book and decided what challenges the main characters faced, then added each sticky note to our chart.

4. The next day, we revisited this chart and repeated the experience with a new book: *Rocket Writes a Story* by Tad Hill.

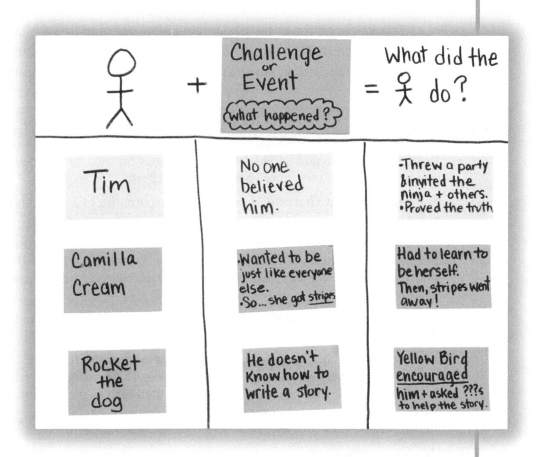

Figure 3.2 *Challenge or Event* chart

Characters, Settings, and Events

This kindergarten chart was created after we read Laura Murray's *The Gingerbread Man Loose in the School*. The literature standard for kindergarten focuses on students being able to identify the characters, events, and locations within stories.

Introducing This Chart:

1. I gathered students and added the three headings on the chart. I spelled and discussed each term after I added it to the chart.

2. You will notice that I have the "s" in *Setting(s)* in parentheses. I used this to point out that a story could have one setting or multiple settings.

3. Before reading out loud, I asked students to listen very closely to the book that I was about to read. I encouraged them to raise their hands if they noticed where the story was set or could identify the characters in the story.

4. As I read, I stopped and called on students who "noticed" either a character or setting. When a student shared one, I wrote it on a sticky note and added it to the chart.

5. After reading the book, we focused on the last column on the chart. As a class, we reconstructed a list of what happened. There are far too many events in books to capture them all on a chart; the goal is to get students to list the events in sequential order.

Book Selections:

Select a book where the settings change frequently. I find that if I use a book with only one or two settings, it can be hard to determine if students really understand what a setting is. You also want to avoid stories that have been retold and are commonly set in the same, easy-to-recall locations. These types of books would include tales like *The Three Little Pigs* or even *The Wizard of Oz*. Some students can guess the location without actively paying attention. You really want to see that students pick up on the shifts and the idea of multiple settings. Laura Murray, Lisa Campbell Ernst, and Kristin Kladstrup all have Gingerbread stories which involve the gingerbread man, girl, or pirate moving through different settings frequently.

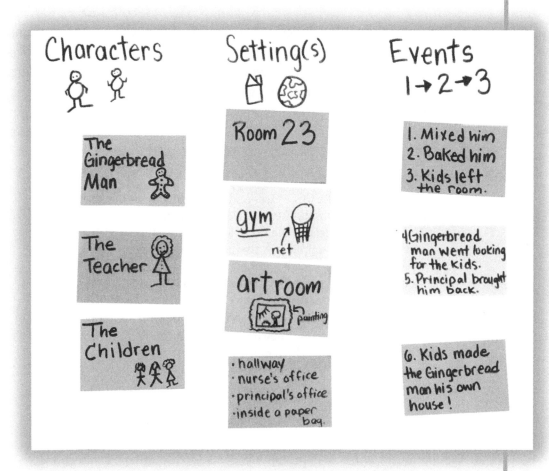

Figure 3.3 *Characters, Settings, and Events* chart

Connections In:

The first grade informational text standard focuses on connections between people, ideas, events, and information within a text. There are dozens of ways to make these types of connections! This chart offers students three simple categories: things that are improvements, challenges, or similarities. These simple categories provide an entryway to begin discussing connections.

Introducing This Chart:

1. For this lesson, I drew the three faces and wrote the title of our read-aloud book on an 8"x6" sticky note. I explained to students that I wanted them to think about the animals in the book and tell how they were related or connected to the other animals in the book. I explained that the happy face was for good, positive, or helpful connections. The angry face was for connections that were bad, difficult, or created challenges. The final two matching faces represented things that were similarities, alike, or the same.

2. The first student example was that "great white whales are connected to people in a good way, because they don't like to eat them" (a fact from the book). I placed that next to the happy face.

3. The second connection was that "all of the animals in the book eat other animals." This showed a similarity among the animals, but it could also be a negative or a challenge for the animals being eaten! Students decided that connections could fit into multiple categories, so we placed that sticky note in between both categories.

4. We continued, with a lot of prompting, and added additional connections to our chart. Afterwards, we reviewed each one.

Books with Easy-to-Spot Connections:

Connections are abstract and challenging for new readers. Try to read texts that feature multiple people and events so that students have a wider array of possible connections.

- *Jackie Robinson* by Wil Mara
- *John, Paul, George, and Ben* by Lane Smith
- *On the Same Day in March: A Tour of the World's Weather* by Marilyn Singer
- *Throw Your Tooth on the Roof: Traditions from Around the World* by Selby Beeler
- *What's Your Favorite Animal?* by Eric Carle
- *Where are All the Night Animals?* by Mary Ann Fraser

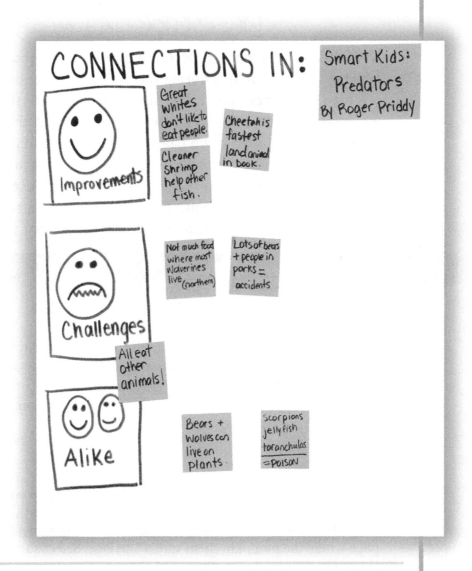

Figure 3.4 *Connections In:* chart

Describe BIG Events

We often ask students to describe events. This happens not just during reading, but also during the course of a school day. How many times have you called students over and asked them to explain or describe what they saw happen on the bus, at the water fountain, or in the hallway? Some students are naturals and provide rich descriptions. Other students just mumble a few words and shut down. Often these students just don't know how to describe an event. This chart provides a set of guiding questions to help all students describe an event from a story.

Introducing This Chart:

I typically read a book out loud, then tell students that I want to talk about one big event from the book. At this point, I draw a boy or girl and call them Mr. or Miss Big Events. I tell students that Mr. Big Events wants to know all about the things that happened in our story. I am very playful with this and slowly write one question at a time. After each question, we discuss the answer as a class. We move on until all of the questions have been addressed.

Teaching Ideas:

- Select a class favorite to reread for this activity. After you read the book, turn back to a page that represents one event in the story. For example, if I read *Cinderella* to my students, I might turn back to the page where the pumpkin turns into a carriage. Select something that is meaningful and has an impact on the direction of the story.

- Fractured fairy tales and post-modern picture books really work well here. These books engage students and the events are easier for students to notice because they stray away from the original events, making them stand out for students. My favorites are *That is Not a Good Idea!* by Mo Willems and *The Three Little Pigs and the Somewhat Bad Wolf* by Mark Teague.

Figure 3.5 *Describe BIG Events chart*

Describing Characters

This is a chart that I have used with all grade levels from kindergarten through eighth grade! Why? The idea of character traits surrounding a character just makes sense! I typically draw a boy on one chart and a girl on a second chart. While I make these charts with my students, I do like to laminate these two charts and reuse them with different books. At the end of the year, I pull two names to see who gets to take one of the charts home. You'd be surprised at the number of students that want to take home either of these charts!

Teaching Ideas:

- When you first introduce this chart, try to select a book with a character that has obvious characteristics that are easy to describe. We described Camilla from David Shannon's *A Bad Case of the Stripes*. Continue to use this chart with increasingly complex characters.

- You can read a book out loud from start to finish first. After reading, ask students to describe the main character as you write their descriptions on sticky notes and add them to the chart.

- Alternatively, you can ask students to raise their hands as soon as they spot a defining characteristic. Then, you can stop and add it to the chart as it happens. I always get many more sticky notes when I add the information while I read the story. This tends to keep students alert and actively listening, but it does result in a lot more noise and requires you to stop and start a lot.

- Place this chart in a center and add a stack of sticky notes nearby. Students can write or draw character traits on the sticky notes and add them to the chart. Then, they can describe the character to a partner or in a small group.

- Dedicate one day a week as Describing Characters Day. On that day, attach the chart to an easel or the chalkboard. Let students dictate or write the character traits that describe one character from their book. To manage this, assign students to specific days. When students get to share, treat it as an honor. Perhaps a student who describes also serves as the line leader or table captain on their Describing Characters Day.

Figure 3.6 *Describing Characters* chart

How Do We Describe Connections?

This chart is specific to the informational text standard for second grade. Students are asked to describe connections between historical events, scientific ideas, or steps in a procedure. To meet the rigor of this standard, students need to have texts that detail historical events, explain scientific ideas, or outline specific steps. These types of texts are most readily connected to science and social studies content.

Creating This Chart:

This chart was created using three 8"x6" sticky notes. I recorded each type of connection on a different sticky note. As I described each one, I drew different images to represent each term. As I state often, I am not the world's best artist, so my images may not be as recognizable to you as they were to my students when I created and explained them. *Historical Events* pictures Abraham Lincoln, a teepee, and a ship. *Scientific Ideas* includes a kite, a light bulb, and a scientific flask. Finally, *Steps in a Procedure* has a staircase and a paper numbered: *1, 2, 3*. The questions in the bubbles were added to help students think about how ideas are connected. These are simply guides and not a strict list of questions that students would need to answer. These are probing questions to encourage students to examine and describe connections.

Teaching Ideas:

1. Instead of focusing on all three types, consider focusing on one at a time. Develop a unit around scientific ideas and focus solely on that before moving on to the others.

2. Relegate historical events to social studies instruction. As you teach your social studies curriculum, make describing connections a part of each unit. This same step can be duplicated with your science curriculum and scientific ideas.

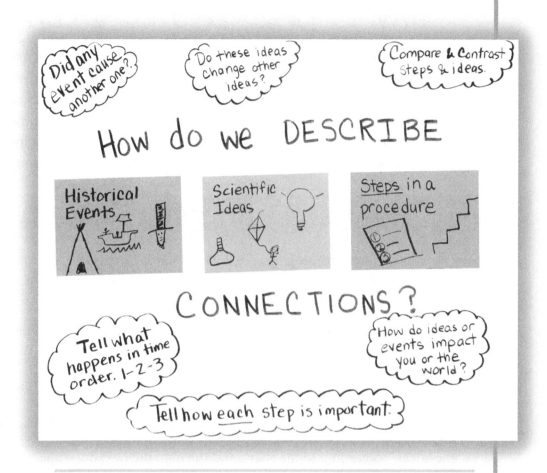

Figure 3.7 *How Do We Describe Connections?* chart

How to Describe the Setting

This chart is aligned to the literature standard. Students are expected to describe the settings in stories. This simple, yet effective, chart provides six concrete questions for students to consider. In the past, I have used variations of these questions and worded them differently. You should feel comfortable changing these questions or adding new ones to suit your instructional needs.

Creating This Chart:

1. I write my questions on large 8"x6" sticky notes in advance, but I don't show them all to my students at the beginning of the lesson.

2. I begin by gathering students on the carpet and adding the title to the chart. Then, I draw a setting on chart paper. I ask students to simply watch and think about what I am drawing.

3. When I finish, I ask students to tell me what season they think this setting is supposed to represent. I am not looking for a specific answer, but I am really listening to their explanations of *why* they picked specific seasons. After we discuss each question, I hold up the sticky note, add it to the chart, and move to the next question.

4. For the question that asks *What can you hear?*, I encourage students to look for clues that can help them determine if there is anything to hear. Be sure to draw an element that could create sound. Smoke from a chimney, a dog, a lightning bolt, and birds are good choices. After you discuss each question, hold it up and add it to the chart.

Figure 3.8 *How to Describe the Setting* chart

Thinking About Characters

This chart helps students with the reading literature standard. The concept is very similar to the *How to Describe the Setting* chart. Instead of asking for a generic description, these guiding questions outline specific aspects to consider when thinking about characters.

Teaching Ideas:

- Search online for pictures of characters that students know well. Display these pictures on the whiteboard. Another option is to use a document camera to project character images directly from books. Ask students to answer each of the questions about the characters, based on what they know. Characters that I have used with students include familiar Dr. Seuss characters, superheroes, Disney characters, fairy tale characters, and David from David Shannon's *No David!*

- Ask students to write a description of a character by responding to each question. It is a good idea to introduce this activity with just one or two sticky notes first, then add more as students get more proficient describing characters.

Writing Connection:

While this is a reading literature standard, students can use this chart for their narrative writing. When students create characters ask them to see if they have answered any of these questions in their writing. For students who struggle to describe characters, this chart also works as an effective scaffold to encourage more description. This chart can also work well when students craft informational/explanatory writing about people. For example, whether students are writing about a best friend, George Washington, or a teacher, they can still refer to these questions to elaborate and describe the person.

Figure 3.9 *Thinking About Characters* chart

3 Types of Connections

This variation of the *Connections In:* chart was created for the kindergarten literature standard. This chart offers a starting point and visual connections as kindergartners begin to think about different ways that ideas and people are connected. This chart is created throughout the school year, introducing one type of connection at a time. I have seen teachers spread these out over three weeks, while others spent months with this.

Teaching Each Connection:

1. For connections that show similarity, hold up classroom objects that are similar (like a blue crayon and a blue chair). Ask students to help you figure out how they are connected or alike. Repeat this with multiple comparisons. Later, move to text and begin looking for similarities.

2. When introducing the happy face connections, consider describing people that are connected to the school, community, or world in a positive way. For example, students might recognize that teachers are connected to students because they help students to learn. Policemen are connected to the community because they keep people safe. Make several of these types of observations to help students conceptualize different types of concrete connections.

3. Finally, for the negative, "uh-oh" connection, focus on things that have causal relationships. Students can discuss how specific actions (events) cause other events. Consider common negative events that students can recognize. Events such as losing recess, time out, or silent lunch are good starting points. *How is silent lunch connected to breaking rules? How is having a temper tantrum connected to time out?* One thing causes another.

4. Students need to conceptualize these connections in real life first. Once students can talk about real-life connections, they will be able to recognize connections within an informational text. Then, they will be ready to move on to books and find more connections on their own.

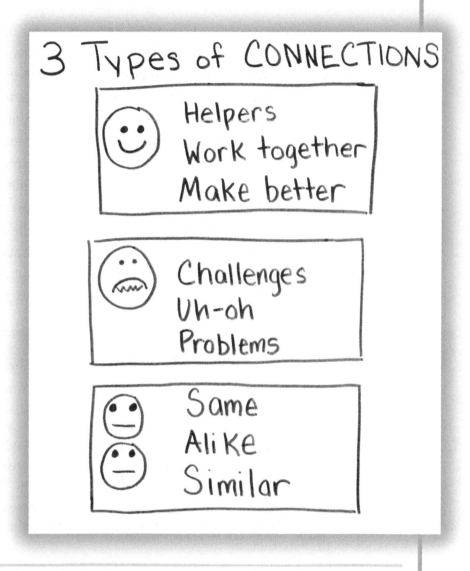

Figure 3.10 *3 Types of Connections* chart

What Are . . .

This chart was created to address the second grade informational text standard. The language of the standard spells out specific things that students should make connections between: *historical events, scientific ideas/concepts,* and *steps in a procedure.* Before addressing the connections, spend time making sure that students can differentiate between these three. This chart displays the three types of topics that an informational text can explore. In this era of testing and accountability, I imagine that standardized reading tests will focus heavily on these three types of topics, since they are specifically spelled out in the standards. Additionally, if students can distinguish between these three things, then they will begin to notice that certain types of connections tend to appear in specific types of texts.

Teaching Ideas:

1. Consider introducing one column at a time or creating individual charts for each one. If you choose to make individual charts, you will have more room to add examples on the chart. In fact, you could even shape the chart to look like the term that it represents. Maybe a light bulb for science, a chart cut into the shape of steps for procedures, and one shaped like the White House for history. Get creative!

2. Send students on a guided scavenger hunt to search for these concepts inside of different books in the class. Gather students together and ask students to share their findings.

3. Collect five or six books that represent each category. Invite students to tour the gallery and discuss what they see.

4. Write book or article titles that fit into the different categories on sticky notes. Add them to the chart or place them around the room, using the wall or a cabinet as an anchor chart for this standard.

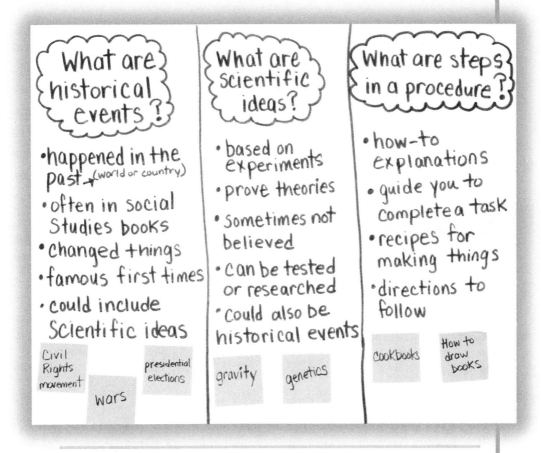

Figure 3.11 *What Are ... chart*

What are Events?

Explaining what an event is to a kindergartner can be hard! To make this task more manageable, I try to give students a few different types of events to consider. The events listed on this chart are not three mutually exclusive or "official" definitions of those events. These definitions all overlap. Events that change the story or help characters learn seem to make sense to students. The first category listed is a catchall for events that do not fit into either of the other categories.

Creating This Chart:

When creating this chart be certain to use as many pictures and symbols as you can. Images also give non-readers more access to the charts. Whenever possible try to pair text with an image. If possible, make your words look like the idea that they represent. Notice how the word "BIG" is actually in larger, capital letters throughout.

Teaching Ideas:

1. Grab a stack of books that you have already read with students and sit down next to an empty chart. Draw each box and discuss with students. Revisit a picture book by asking students to think about the major events that changed the story or helped the characters to learn. Write these responses on sticky notes and place them under each box. You could even begin by asking students to think of events from movies, fairy tales, and class read-alouds. Add the different events to the chart and discuss.

2. Focus on one category at a time. Then, read books that focus on mostly the same types of events. For example, you could build an entire unit around books where the characters learn. This pairs nicely with the concept of lessons and morals (literature standard two).

3. Take one book and identify several events yourself. Share each event and ask students to discuss why that event is important to the story.

What are events?

The BIG things that happen!

- Stella loses her book!
- Crayons were angry
- Max is in the forest
- Wizard with no magic!

BIG things that help to learn.

- Camilla's Stripes
- Little Bird's questions
- Monster sharing

BIG things that CHANGE change the story.

- Fairy Godmother
- Jack climbed up the beanstalk
- Snow White bites the apple.
- Wolf couldn't blow down the house

Figure 3.12 *What are Events?* chart

What is a Character?

This a great chart to introduce students to the terminology of the literature standard. Create this chart with any grade level as an introduction or as a reinforcement of prior learning. Be certain to include images for each box. These images help students to remember and differentiate between the ideas.

Creating This Chart:

I create this chart by simply writing the title of the chart and asking students to tell me what a character is. After a brief discussion, I draw the image and write the words on the chart. Then, I share a short, easy-to-read book that features clearly defined characters. If you have limited time, consider reading an excerpt, or you can simply flip through a few pages of the book so that students can have a good look at the characters. I repeat this for each box. Try reading a Shel Silverstein poem from *Where the Sidewalk Ends* and ask students to tell you about those characters. As students become more proficient, consider moving to increasingly complex text.

Shel Silverstein Poems with Memorable Characters:

- "Me and My Giant"
- "Sick"
- "The Crocodile's Toothache"
- "The Long-Haired Boy"

Short Picture Books with Memorable Characters:

- *A Bad Case of the Stripes* by David Shannon
- *David Gets in Trouble* by David Shannon
- *Gingerbread Baby* by Jan Brett
- *Little Red Writing* by Joan Holub
- *Wilma Jean the Worry Machine* by Julia Cook

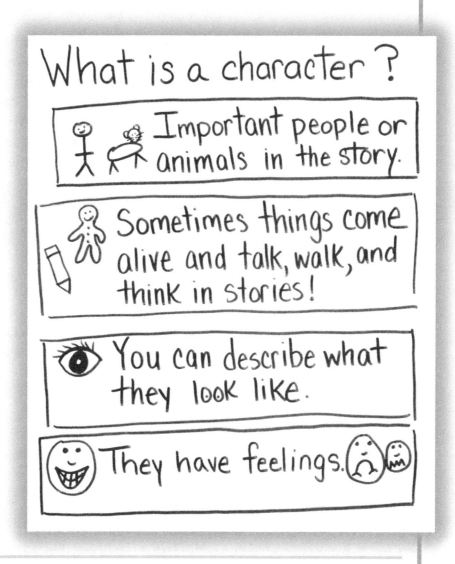

Figure 3.13 *What is a Character?* chart

What is a Setting?

This simple chart is really about helping students consider different ways to describe story settings. I like to move to this chart when students have already had instruction on setting as a location. Instead of just naming the setting, students can begin to situate it. Instead of being set in the jungle, now a book is set in the jungle on a hot day. Students begin to grasp that settings help paint pictures for the readers, not just name a location.

Teaching Ideas:

- Read books that show changes in time and weather. Ask students to explain how the setting changes and the impact that it has on the characters.

- Each time you discuss a book's setting, add it to the bottom of the chart. Let students have a visual for the books that they know and can talk about.

- Place sticky notes at the bottom that name different types of weather or time descriptions. Words like *rainy, blizzard, hot, freezing,* and *windy* will help students begin to think about the different aspects of settings.

Picture Books Where Weather or Time of Day is Explicit:

- *Cloudy with a Chance of Meatballs* by Judi Barrett
- *Pickles to Pittsburgh* by Judi Barrett
- *Day it Rained Hearts* by Felicia Bond
- *Kitten's First Full Moon* by Kevin Henkes
- *The Night Before Kindergarten* by Natasha Wing
- *Room on the Broom* by Julia Donaldson
- *Snow Rabbit, Spring Rabbit* by Il Sung Na

Picture Books that Show Multiple Setting Locations:

- *Fancy Nancy* by Jane O'Connor *(eight settings)*
- *Green Eggs and Ham* by Dr. Seuss
- *Stick Man* by Julia Donaldson
- *Stella Louella's Runway Book* by Lisa Campbell Ernst
- *Journey* by Aaron Becker *(wordless)*

Figure 3.14 *What is a Setting?* chart

What Settings Do We Know?

Often we simply tell students what a *story element* is. Story elements are not necessarily engaging to think about. Most readers (me, included) just want to hear or read a great story. To get students just as interested in the story elements, it is necessary to introduce the elements individually, connect them to the real world, and then tie them back to books.

Introducing This Chart:

1. I tell students that there is a cool, new kindergarten word for the world around them. The *setting* tells where you are. It can include the time, date, and place.

2. After explaining this term, I write the title of the chart and ask students to think of places where they have been before. I list the settings as students share them, stopping to draw a picture next to each one. These images will help students visualize the different settings.

3. Then, I read a book that includes one of the settings on our list. Students always include the classroom or home on this list, so a book set in either of these places works well.

4. After I read the book, I create a sticky note for the book title and place it next to the settings that were found in that book. To help my new readers, I photocopy the book cover, shrink it down to about 35% of the original size, wrap packing tape around it (for lamination) and place it on the chart.

5. Throughout the year, I continue to add more books to this chart and tell students to be on the lookout for settings like these within books.

6. The chart pictured here is the original chart and students had yet to add different titles. This is what your chart would look like at the beginning of the year. As you add the names or photocopies of book covers, the chart would slowly fill up. By the end of the year, this chart could be completely filled.

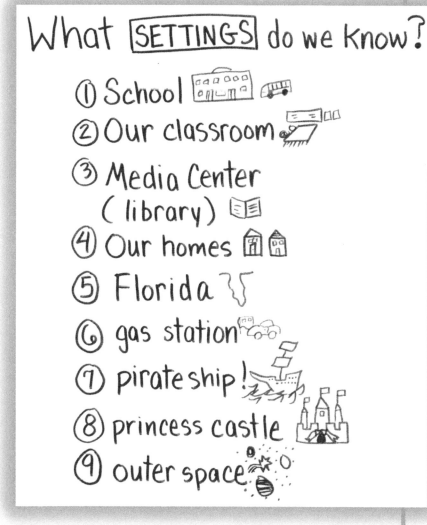

What **SETTINGS** do we know?

1. School
2. Our classroom
3. Media Center (library)
4. Our homes
5. Florida
6. gas station
7. pirate ship!
8. princess castle
9. outer space

Figure 3.15 *What Settings Do We Know?* chart

Chapter 4

Word Play

Common Core Reading Anchor Standard 4:
Interpret words and phrases as they are used in a text, including determining technical, connotative, and figurative meanings, and analyze how specific word choices shape meaning or tone.

	Literary Text	Informational Text
K	Ask and answer questions about unknown words in a text.	With prompting and support, ask and answer questions about unknown words in a text.
1	Identify words and phrases in stories or poems that suggest feelings or appeal to the senses.	Ask and answer questions to help determine or clarify the meaning of words and phrases in a text.
2	Describe how words and phrases (e.g., regular beats, alliteration, rhymes, repeated lines) supply rhythm and meaning in a story, poem, or song.	Determine the meanings of words and phrases in a text relevant to a grade 2 topic or subject area.

Look for Alliteration

This chart is a great introduction to alliteration. Beforehand, select a set of books that contain alliteration. I like for students to be able to look through different books and find examples of alliteration after we create this chart together. An alternative is to select poems with alliteration. Any Shel Silverstein book will offer numerous poems filled with alliteration.

Introducing This Chart:

Typically, I call a student to the front of the room and add an adjective to his or her name. So Shellie becomes Smart Shellie, Marty becomes Marvelous Marty, etc. After each student is given an alliterative name, I ask students what they notice about their new names. I then introduce the term *alliteration* and explain what it means. At this point, I create the bubble with the chart title. Next, I spread the books out for students to look through, then send them on a mission to find examples of alliteration and write them down. You could also ask students to record the book and page number or place a sticky note on the pages that feature alliteration. After ten or fifteen minutes, I group students together on the carpet, and we share the examples that we found. We discuss each one and I post several on the chart.

Texts with Alliteration:

- *Double Trouble in Walla Walla* by Andrew Clements
- *Four Fur Feet* by Margaret Wise Brown
- *Henry and the Buccaneer Bunnies* by Carolyn Crimi
- *Lilly's Purple Plastic Purse* by Kevin Henkes
- *Princess Prunella and the Purple Peanut* by Margaret Atwood
- *Rude Ramsay and the Roaring Radishes* by Margaret Atwood
- *Some Smug Slug* by Pamela Duncan Edwards
- *Tikki Tikki Tembo* by Arlene Mosel
- *Velma Gratch and the Way Cool Butterfly* by Alan Madison

Figure 4.1 *Look for Alliteration* chart

Solving Unknown Words

Students will always encounter unfamiliar words. Unfortunately, many students have no idea what to do when this happens. Some students shut down, others panic, and many stop reading at that point. This chart is a quick reference list of strategies that students can turn to when this happens. This chart was created with second graders, but can be adapted for younger students by adding images to represent the different strategies.

Introducing This Chart:

I introduce this chart by asking students if they have ever encountered tricky words in a book before. We share a few experiences that we have had with challenging words. Next, I write the title on the chart. In a simple conversational style, I explain each strategy and add it to the chart. These strategies are not static and can be replaced or altered in any way. When students come to me and ask what a word means, I direct them to this chart and ask which strategies they have already tried. For students who are reluctant to try new strategies, I guide them through different options and coach them through some of the choices.

Teaching Ideas:

- Consider writing the different strategies on large 8"x6" sticky notes. This will allow you to swap out different choices, as needed, and move sticky notes around to accommodate additional strategies.

- Introduce this chart with text that contains challenging vocabulary. Display the text on a whiteboard and read aloud. Model how you use the different strategies with the text excerpt.

- Create a signal for students to indicate whenever they use one of the strategies. Some teachers have used a bell, Popsicle® sticks, hand signals, or small sticky notes that students add to the chart next to the strategy that they relied on.

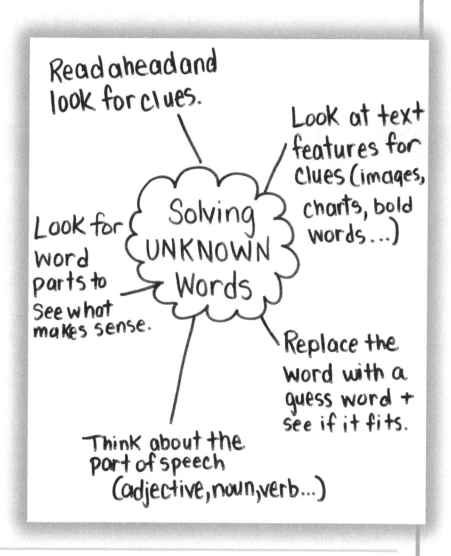

Figure 4.2 *Solving Unknown Words* chart

Stories, Songs, and Poems

The second grade literature standard focuses on recognizing how words and phrases contribute to the meaning and rhythm of a song, story, or poem. This chart is an introduction to this terminology.

Introducing This Chart:

I added the title to this chart and asked students if they had any favorite stories, songs, or poems that they could share with the class. After sharing a few of these out loud, I tell students that each of these has a rhythm. This is a great opportunity to clap a beat or rhythm with students. I am quite musically challenged, so I usually just clap out the syllables to students' names and encourage them to clap along. A more rhythmic option would be to clap out more complex beats or even play a song and clap along with the rhythm or to the beat. After clapping the syllables, I write the rest of the chart and explain each word. Next, I introduce each sticky note as a vocabulary word, adding examples to each one.

Teaching Ideas:

1. Share a poem that represents alliteration, rhyming words, beats, and repeated lines. My favorites are always Shel Silverstein poems. I often choose his work due to the sheer quantity and accessibility. A few of his books can yield hundreds of great options that never disappoint. For second grade teachers, investing in a few of his titles is worth it!

2. Consider adding the sticky notes over time. You could teach a much more elaborate lesson for each concept and build the chart over several days.

3. Select several poems and ask students to color code or underline different elements that they find in the poetry. This could be a whole group scavenger hunt or students could work in teams.

Figure 4.3 *Stories, Songs, and Poems chart*

Stuck on a Word? Take 5!

This chart is a simple resource to help students remember to rely on strategies when they get stuck on a tricky word. This list can be expanded or changed as needed to meet the needs of your students.

Introducing This Chart:

I direct students to revisit this chart when they encounter a tricky word during independent reading. If a student comes to me and asks what a word means, I walk to the chart with him or her and ask which one of the strategies we should try first. I guide them through the steps and help them to solve the word. Once you have done this a few times, students will begin to move to this step on their own.

Teaching Ideas:

- Model how to use these strategies with students. I like to begin with a simple text and pretend to be confused about a well-known word. Students usually just want to shout out the word and help me. Instead, I pretend not to hear the word-callers, and actively think out loud, using each strategy. Not only are students tickled, but they get a chance to see the strategy in action.

- Ask students to add other strategies that they have used to solve words. Write these ideas on sticky notes and add them to the chart as well.

- Don't recreate the wheel! If you use a specific phonics or vocabulary series, use the terminology found in those books on your chart. I know that many teachers rely on reading strategy cards that name word attack strategies like *Stretch the Snake* or *Skippy the Skip It Frog*. If your school uses those labels, incorporate them here on your chart.

Figure 4.4 *Stuck on a Word? Take 5!* chart

Vote for the Best Rhyme!

This chart is designed for the second grade literature standard, but can easily be used in any grade level. To create this, I read a passage from my favorite book of poetry, *Where the Sidewalk Ends* by Shel Silverstein. Any poem or poetry book can work just as well.

Introducing This Chart:

I read the poem "Sick" out loud to students, stopping periodically to question, reread parts, and elicit student commentary. After reading the poem, I use a document camera to project the poem overhead. You could also project an online version on the screen. I ask students to find the best rhyming lines in the poem. They are asked to write the lines down and be prepared to share. We discuss the rhymes and I read each one, pointing out the rhyming words. Then, I select four passages from the poem. These are the four that I record on the chart. Next, I ask students to talk with a partner about which is the best rhyme. The whole point of this is to get students to read (and talk about) multiple rhyming lines. Finally, we vote on which rhyme from "Sick" is the best one. I tally the votes on the chart and we declare that rhyme as the winner.

Teaching Ideas:

1. Repeat this activity with additional poems, then display the charts around the classroom. Encourage students to "read the room" when they finish other work.

2. Challenge students to create their own poems that feature rhyming words as well. Post these alongside poems written by professional writers.

3. Create a chart of rhyming words for students to reference and use in their writing. Fill this chart with rhyming words from actual poems. This will yield a much richer and complex list than just listing random rhyming words. As a result you will have pairings such as *Saturday* and *play* instead of *bat* and *cat*.

Figure 4.5 *Vote for the Best Rhyme!* chart

Ways to Add Rhythm

This chart features the vocabulary of the second grade literature standard. This chart uses the terminology of the standard, matches each term to an image, and lists specific texts that model these features.

Introducing This Chart:

I like to play music when I introduce this chart. Good choices are instrumental versions of popular songs or even nursery rhymes. After the music plays for a while, I turn it down and tell the students that songs have different rhythms, rhymes, and beats. Music is not the only place to find these elements. Books and poems can also have different beats and rhythm. Then, I write each box on the chart and discuss it. After our discussion, I read a poem or story that includes one of the features. Note that the names of several books with these features are posted on sticky notes at the bottom of the chart.

Teaching Ideas:

- Create this chart over time. Introduce one or two elements during a class period. Slowly move on as students show mastery of each concept.
- Instead of reading the books out loud, gather a collection of books with these features and ask students to use sticky notes to tag different passages that show alliteration, beats, rhymes, or repeated lines. Gather students together and have them share what they've found.
- Play multiple songs with clear beats and rhymes. A great website (at the time of publication) with a wide variety of songs categorized in different ways is: http://bethsmusicnotes.blogspot.com/.
- Connect this skill to writing. Help students to craft their own short poems that include these different features. After students share their work with the class, call on different students to identify what elements they noticed in each other's writing.

Figure 4.6 *Ways to Add Rhythm* chart

Why Do Authors Repeat Lines?

This chart works well with the second grade reading standard. Instead of just listing the terminology, this chart addresses why repeated lines are useful in literature. I offer students two distinctly different reasons, along with a third reason (which is really a combination of the first two reasons).

Introducing This Chart:

I write the title of this chart and lead a discussion about what *repeated lines* are. I explain that repeated lines can be one line followed by the same exact line or the same line repeated at intervals throughout the text. Then, I add the three boxes to the chart, stopping to clarify words such as *emphasis, emphasize,* and *phrase.* I typically read a poem or short story to model each of the chart categories. After reading each poem or book, I write the book title on a sticky note and add it to the chart. The next day, I read additional titles and we continue to grow this chart over time.

Texts that Feature Repeated Lines:

- "Boa Constrictor" in *Where the Sidewalk Ends* by Shel Silverstein
- *Chicka Chicka Boom Boom* by Bill Martin and John Archambault
- *Five Little Monkeys Jumping on the Bed* by Eileen Christelow
- *I'm Gonna Like Me: Letting Off a Little Self-Esteem* by Jamie Lee Curtis
- "Lazy Jane" in *Where the Sidewalk Ends* by Shel Silverstein
- *No, David!* by David Shannon
- *What Will Hatch?* by Jennifer Ward
- *Who Has Seen the Wind?* by Christina Rossetti

Figure 4.7 *Why Do Authors Repeat Lines?* chart

Word Detectives

This word-solving chart was created with kindergartners, but is effective with any grade level. When I create this chart with students, I like to dress up as a detective. At my best, I don a full beige trench coat, deerstalker hat, and magnifying glass. I love to pass out tiny magnifying glasses to the students as well. Other times, I simply have my magnifying glass and tell students that I am a detective. Consider dressing as a detective when you create this chart with your readers.

Introducing This Chart:

I tell students that I am a detective looking for clues. I ask my fellow "detectives" to stand up and follow me. We form a conga-style line and proceed to walk around the classroom eyeing different objects with our magnifying glasses. Students begin to ask what we are looking for. Finally, I come back to the carpet and tell students that we are all word detectives. Most students look confused or laugh. I explain that in kindergarten we will run into words that we don't know or understand. Good word detectives have to figure out what those words mean. At this point, I draw and introduce each strategy, placing it on our anchor chart. Then, I call on students to use their magnifying glass to name the strategy that they plan to use first when they run into a tricky word. I call on every student, if possible, just to have students read and name each strategy multiple times.

Teaching Idea:

After you create this chart, try to model these strategies every day. If you do a daily read-aloud, this is a perfect time to model the strategies. While reading, pretend to get stuck on a word. After expressing your confusion, turn to this chart and name a strategy to try. Then, think aloud and model how you use the strategy.

Figure 4.8 *Word Detectives* chart

Words Show Emotions

This chart helps students to understand that words can communicate emotions. While this seems like a simple idea, many students have never explicitly been taught this. The goal for this chart is to make this concept tangible and concrete for students.

Introducing This Chart:

1. I begin by asking students to name an emotion. I call on multiple students to identify different emotions.

2. Next, I ask students how different emotions look. What does *sad* look like? What does *angry* look like? I ask for volunteers to stand up and demonstrate different emotions. I call attention to the movements and expressions that students rely on to show these emotions. For example, I might point out that Phillip stomped his feet to show anger or that Sara wiped her eyes to show sadness.

3. After we have acted out several emotions, I explain that books can show emotion with words.

4. I create the chart and draw the faces for three or four emotions. For this chart, I chose *happiness, sadness,* and *anger.*

5. Finally, I read a few books out loud. I ask the students to stop me when they hear a word or clue that shows emotion. Each time a student stops me, I reread that sentence and we discuss what emotion the text shows.

Picture Books with Emotional Words:

- *Alexander and the Terrible, Horrible, No Good, Very Bad Day* by Judith Viorst
- *David Gets in Trouble* by David Shannon
- *I Love My Hair* by Natasha Anastasia Tarpley
- *Pink Tiara Cookies for Three* by Maria Dismondy
- *Princess Hyacinth* by Florence Parry Heide
- *Thank You Mr. Falker* by Patricia Pollaco
- *The Day the Crayons Quit* by Drew Daywalt
- *When Sophie Gets Angry—Really, Really Angry* by Molly Bang

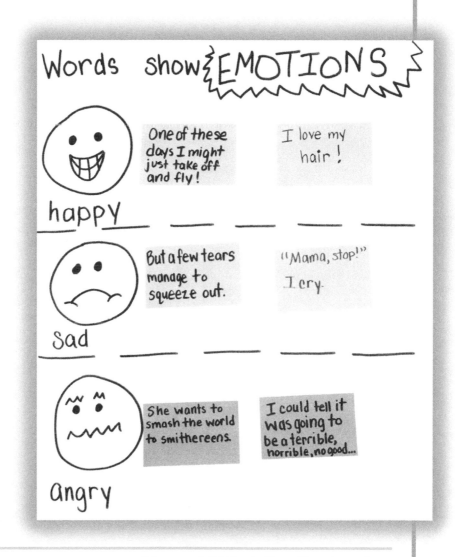

Figure 4.9 *Words Show Emotions* chart

Chapter 5

Text Features

Common Core Reading Anchor Standard 5:
Analyze the structure of texts, including how specific sentences, paragraphs, and larger portions of the text (e.g., a section, chapter, scene, or stanza) relate to each other and the whole.

	Literary Text	Informational Text
K	Recognize common types of texts (e.g., storybooks, poems).	Identify the front cover, back cover, and title page of a book.
1	Explain major differences between books that tell stories and books that give information, drawing on a wide reading of a range of text types.	Know and use various text features (e.g., headings, tables of contents, glossaries, electronic menus, icons) to locate key facts or information in a text.
2	Describe the overall structure of a story, including describing how the beginning introduces the story and the ending concludes the action.	Know and use various text features (e.g., captions, bold print, subheadings, glossaries, indexes, electronic menus, icons) to locate key facts or information in a text efficiently.

Match the Text Feature

This interactive chart can be used to describe different text features and serve as a matching game. The four text features pictured here are from the first grade informational text standard. Review your grade-level standards for specific features that you may want to include.

Creating This Chart:

I wrote the names and descriptions of different text features on 8"x6" sticky notes and placed each of them on the wall. On smaller 4"x4" sticky notes I wrote phrases like: *love it, you rock,* and *not so sure.* I placed these to the side of the larger sticky notes.

Matching Game Rules:

To play the matching game, write the title on the chart and write the names of four (or more) different text features on sticky notes. Tell students that when you call on them, they will have one minute to find the matching description and place it on the chart, next to the name of the feature. After a student makes their matches, call on two other students to check if the matches are correct. Students can use the smaller sticky notes to indicate if the match is correct. Students can take turns and play repeatedly. Change out the terms regularly.

Teaching Ideas:

- Make this a center by placing the sticky notes on a wall. Challenge students to work in groups to unscramble the words and descriptions.

- As you introduce each feature, use the whiteboard to display a text example of each feature.

- Encourage students to look for examples of different features when they read independently. When students recognize a feature in a book or online article, write the name of the feature on a small sticky note and place it on the wall or on a chart dedicated to collecting text features.

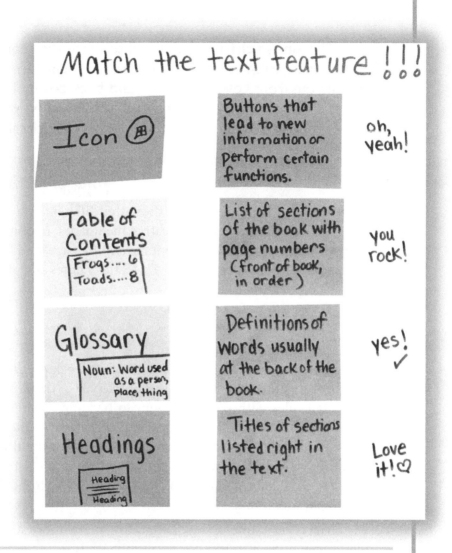

Figure 5.1 *Match the Text Feature* chart

Parts of a Book

This simple chart was created to meet the requirements of the kindergarten literature standard. Students are expected to identify the front cover, title page, and back cover. This is a great chart to use during the first week of school when you introduce students to the media center and your classroom library.

Creating This Chart:

I simply held up picture books to show the different features before drawing them on the chart. After creating the images, I pointed out elements that were included on the front cover, title page, and back cover. Then, I wrote these features on small 4"x4" sticky notes and placed them under each of the three sections.

Teaching Ideas:

- Revisit this chart each day during the first week of school. Gather students together and review the book parts. Then, ask students to switch roles with you. Tell them to become teachers. Ask each student to select a book and find the three parts. Then, they can trade places with you and "teach" the class about the three parts of their book. Consider sitting on the carpet while each student sits in the teacher's chair or stands in front of the room to hold up his or her book, explaining each part.

- My chart is very simple; consider adding many more sticky notes to elaborate on the elements found in each section.

- Some teachers have used a color copier to photocopy the front and back covers of actual picture books, and then added these to the chart in lieu of the drawings. This is a creative choice that is visually appealing.

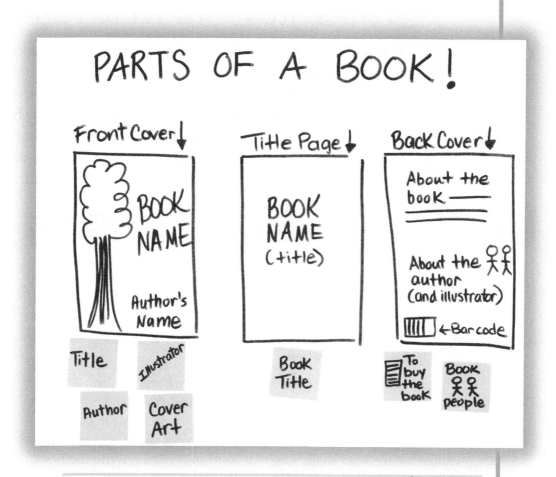

Figure 5.2 *Parts of a Book* chart

Stories Take You on a Ride!

The second grade literature standard states that students should be able to recognize the overall structure of a story, specifically understanding the role of the beginning and ending. There are several options for introducing this concept. One way to teach this is to name the beginning, middle, and end of a text. Another option is to utilize more traditional story structure words and name the plot and climax, or even problem and solution.

Teaching Ideas:

- Introduce this chart by asking students if they have been on any amusement park rides before. Let students demonstrate how it felt when they were on the Ferris wheel or carousel. After engaging students, link this feeling to how it feels when you read a good book. Then, draw the rollercoaster and the rollercoaster cars with descriptions of each section.

- After creating this chart, complete a short art and reading activity. Give each student a short book on their reading level. Cut colored construction paper into rectangles and give one to each student. Then, let students glue on black circles to represent wheels. After students have read their book out loud to a friend, write the book title on their railroad car. Connect the cars to one another to create a chain of rollercoaster cars that form a train around the room.

- Read a book aloud as you create the chart. Stop when one of the descriptions occurs in the book. For example, as soon as you meet the characters, stop and point that out, then add "meet characters" to the chart. Continue through the book, periodically stopping to observe and add more features.

Figure 5.3 *Stories Take You on a Ride!* chart

Stories vs. Informational Text

The first grade informational text standard is really about differentiating between informational text and literature. I create this Venn diagram and explain the differences between these two types of text. Then, I read several stories and informational texts out loud. After each book, I ask students to tell me which clues helped them to decide if the book was an informational text or a story. I write the book names on sticky notes and add them to the bottom of the chart.

Informational Text or Nonfiction?

At first glance, it seems as though this is the same as comparing fiction to nonfiction. In reality, it is a bit different. Informational text actually includes books that traditionally have been considered fiction. Strong examples of books that teeter on the line between fiction and nonfiction are Joanna Cole's *Magic School Bus* books. These types of blended books are classified as informational text even though the characters are imaginary. This type of blended writing seems to be an emerging trend that is gaining popularity. For this standard, I avoid reading blended informational texts when I first introduce the two genres. After students understand the traits of each genre, then I introduce the blended books as informational text that "steals" some of the characteristics of stories. When I read the blended informational texts to students, we name the features that are more associated with stories and the ones that are more associated with informational text.

Blended Informational Texts:

- *It's Back to School We Go!* by Ellen Jackson
- *Leonardo and the Flying Boy* by Laurence Anholt
- *My Best Friend, Abe Lincoln* by Robert Bloch
- *Picasso and the Girl with a Ponytail* by Laurence Anholt
- *Snowflake Bentley* by Jacqueline Briggs Martin
- *Stellaluna* by Janell Cannon
- *The Magic School Bus* series by Joanna Cole

Figure 5.4 *Stories vs. Informational Text* chart

Text Features

This is a basic chart that matches the name of a text feature to an image of that feature. The terms included on this chart come directly from the second grade informational text standard, but any terms can be used when creating a chart like this.

Introducing This Chart:

I introduce each of these features while reading an informational text to students. If you don't have many informational text titles, turn to your social studies or science books. These types of texts include an abundance of text features. The *Time for Kids* website (www.timeforkids.com) is also a great source for informational text. This site offers a wide variety of online articles that showcase lots of subheadings and captions. There is even a tab on the menu called *Photos and Videos* that leads to hundreds of images with very detailed captions.

Teaching Ideas:

- This chart can be modified in many ways. Consider cutting out magazine pictures or old book pages that represent each of the features. Use these real images in place of the drawings.

- Ask students to draw the different features and use those drawings on the chart.

- Make this chart interactive! Write the names, pictures, and descriptions on large 8"x6" sticky notes. Students can remove, sort, and match the images to the correct name and definition.

- Make the connection to writing. Encourage students to incorporate some of these features into their own informational writing. A fun way to do this is to assign headings such as *birthplace, favorites, family,* etc. Have students use the headings to craft autobiographies. Require students to include multiple text features in these pieces.

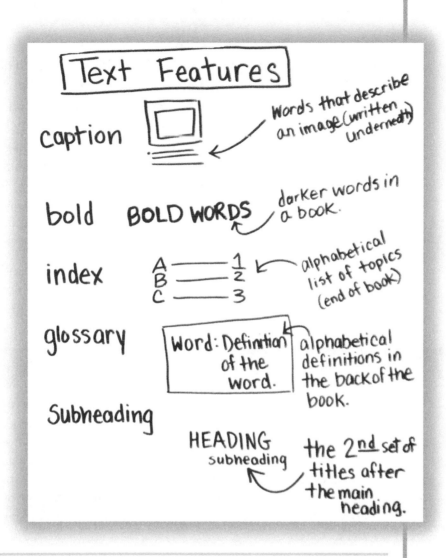

Text Features

caption — Words that describe an image (written underneath)

bold — **BOLD WORDS** — darker words in a book.

index — A ═ 1, B ═ 2, C ─ 3 — alphabetical list of topics (end of book)

glossary — Word: Definition of the word. — alphabetical definitions in the back of the book.

Subheading — HEADING subheading — the 2nd set of titles after the main heading.

Figure 5.5 *Text Features* chart

Two Types of Literature

This chart is aligned to the kindergarten literature standard, but was created with a small group of second grade students. These students didn't know the differences between the two types of literature. They simply thought one was shorter. Before moving forward to dissecting stories, we took a step back and taught students the skills that they had missed. To adapt this for kindergarten, use images and single words to represent the characteristics of each type of literature. The word *short* can replace the first bullet under *poems,* followed by a musical note to represent *rhythm,* etc.

Vertical Alignment:

It is important to be aware of the standards that precede and follow your own grade level. Use this information to reteach or fill academic gaps, or as a guide to accelerate learning for students who are ready to move forward.

Introducing This Chart:

1. I shared several poems from my favorite poetry book, *Where the Sidewalk Ends* by Shel Silverstein. Then, I shifted gears and read *My Name is Not Isabella* by Jennifer Fosberry. This book is a story, but contains great biographical information about famous women from history. It really straddles the fence between informational text and literature. Because the information about the women is very limited throughout the actual story, I still treat it as literature. For this activity, any engaging story will work.

2. After reading, I asked the students to think about the differences between the text in *Where the Sidewalk Ends* and *My Name is Not Isabella.*

3. While students looked back through the two books together, I drew the two boxes and labeled each side.

4. I listed the differences that students noted and even used this opportunity to introduce the term *alliteration.*

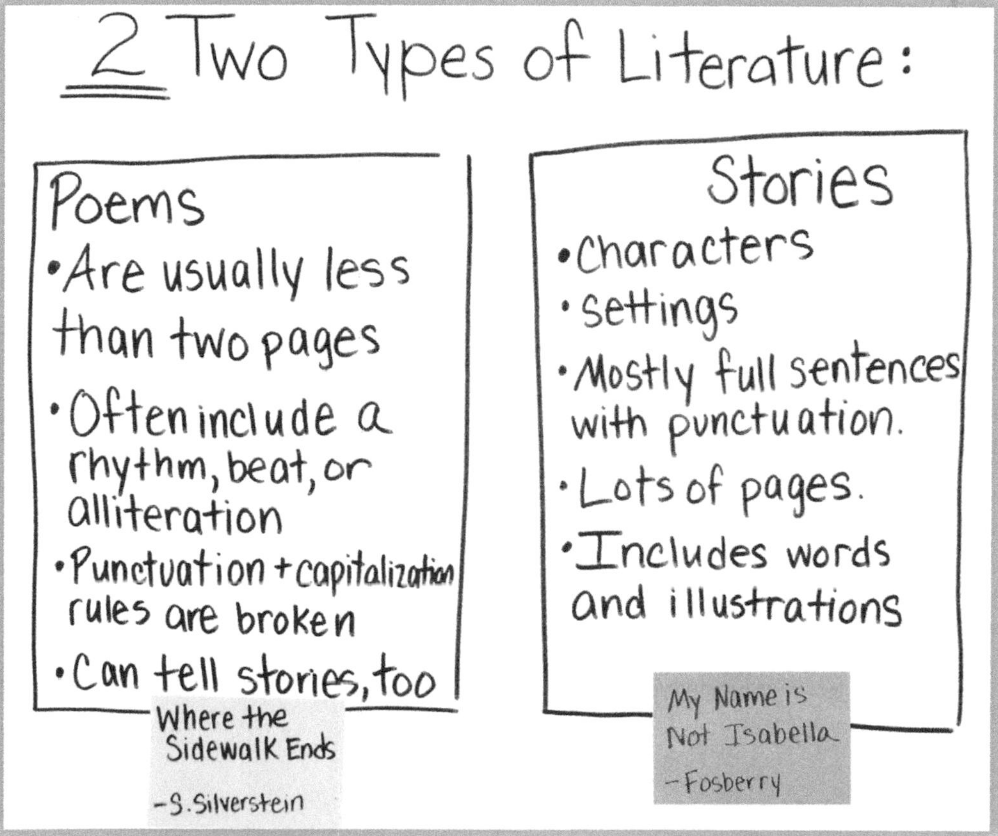

2 Two Types of Literature:

Poems
- Are usually less than two pages
- Often include a rhythm, beat, or alliteration
- Punctuation + capitalization rules are broken
- Can tell stories, too

Where the Sidewalk Ends

−S. Silverstein

Stories
- Characters
- Settings
- Mostly full sentences with punctuation.
- Lots of pages.
- Includes words and illustrations

My Name is Not Isabella

−Fosberry

Figure 5.6 *Two Types of Literature* chart

Chapter 6

Authors, Illustrators, and Narrators

Common Core Reading Anchor Standard 6:
Assess how point of view or purpose shapes the content and style of a text.

	Literary Text	Informational Text
K	With prompting and support, name the author and illustrator of a story and define the role of each in telling the story.	Name the author and illustrator of a text and define the role of each in presenting the ideas or information in a text.
1	Identify who is telling the story at various points in a text.	Distinguish between information provided by pictures or other illustrations and information provided by the words in a text.
2	Acknowledge differences in points of view of characters, including by speaking in a different voice for each character when reading dialogue aloud.	Identify the main purpose of a text, including what the author wants to answer, explain, or describe.

Authors/Illustrators

Created over several days, this chart meets the rigor of the kindergarten literature standard. Students are expected to identify and understand the role of authors and illustrators.

Introducing This Chart:

- Before drawing the chart, I read two picture books to the class. We read *Big Bad Bubble* and *Dragons Love Tacos,* both written by Adam Rubin and illustrated by Daniel Salmieri. After reading both books, I explained that these books were created by two people. One person drew the pictures and the other person made up the story and wrote the words. Holding up both covers, I pointed to and spelled the name of each person.

- Then, I drew the two boxes on the chart and added the headings. We talked about Adam and Daniel and what we liked about their work, leafing back through parts of the book. I called on students to point out words that Adam wrote and images that Daniel drew. After our discussion, I added two 8"x6" sticky notes to the chart and wrote both names on them. I deliberately put Adam's name underneath illustrator and Daniel's name underneath author. The students shouted and told me that I had it wrong. I asked why and called on students to explain the role of each person and switched the sticky notes to the correct positions.

- Over the next two days, I repeated this same process with books by different authors and illustrators. Finally, I read *Don't Let the Pigeon Drive the Bus* and *We Are in a Book!* by Mo Willems. I save Mo Willems for the end because he is one of the growing number of authors who do their own illustrations. I wanted students to see that many authors do both.

Ten Authors Who Illustrate Their Own Picture Books:

1. Barney Saltzberg
2. Don Freeman
3. Dr. Seuss
4. Eric Carle
5. Janell Cannon
6. Kevin Henkes
7. Linda Kranz
8. Maurice Sendak
9. Mo Willems
10. Oliver Jeffers

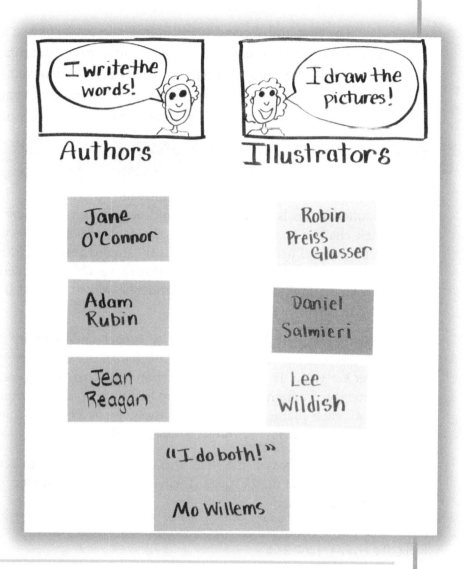

Figure 6.1 *Authors/Illustrators* chart

Characters Have Different Points of view

The first and second grade literature standards are actually fun standards that are enjoyable to teach and engage students. Students are expected to read with different voices when different characters are speaking. This is the precursor to understanding that there are different points of view and different types of narration.

Introducing This Chart:

1. I began by displaying several different "characters." I have used stuffed animals, Lego® people, old action figures, finger puppets, felt characters, and paper dolls. The goal is to select very different characters. I used a Paddington Bear™ stuffed animal, a Barbie™ doll, and a stuffed alligator. I placed all three on a table and asked students to take a look at the table. As students walked around the table, I wrote the title on the chart.

2. Next, I gathered students on the carpet and held up the three characters. *Guys, how do you think Barbie speaks? Can anyone act out her voice?* This caused laughter and excitement. Several students attempted a high-pitched, overtly feminine voice. We repeated this with each character. After our activity, we agreed that characters in books should have different voices as well.

3. I drew the faces on the chart and called on students to act out how each character might speak. Then, I added the four sentences and the speech bubble.

Teaching Ideas:

- Specify that *different* voices and *distracting* voices are not the same thing. I did have to explain this to several students who just wanted to shout or be overtly silly.

- You may want to model four or five different voices yourself. Some students struggled to create different voices and needed some tips on how to do this in a sustainable way.

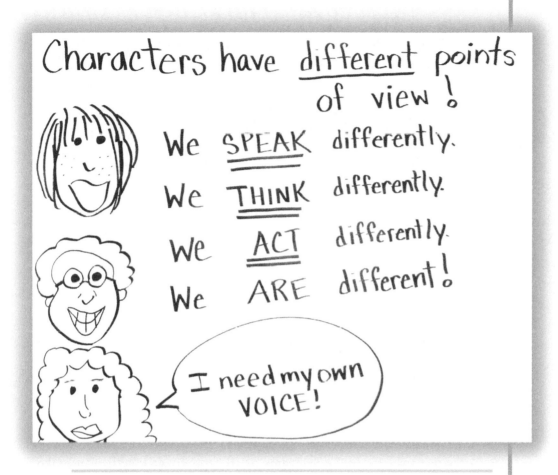

Figure 6.2 *Characters Have Different Points of View* chart

Different Character Voices

This simple chart was created with kindergartners. This chart targets the struggling readers and includes more symbols to represent text than some of the other charts.

Creating This Chart:

1. I placed the three smaller sticky notes on the chart and read each one. I asked students if we all had the same thoughts. We discussed how different we all are. We repeated this discussion with each of the three statements. You can use different statements here. The point is that your students talk about some differences between people and characters.

2. After our discussion, I drew the equal sign and added the large speech bubble. The speech bubble is written on a huge 11"x11" sticky note.

3. Next, I held up the traditional story of *The Three Little Pigs* by Patricia Seibert. I asked students what type of voices I should use for the pigs and the wolf. They wanted a scary, loud voice for the wolf and softer voices for the pigs.

4. After reading the traditional story, I held up *The Three Little Wolves and the Big Bad Pig* by Eugene Trivizas. This time the types of voices that were suggested switched and the pig became the character with the harsher, much louder voice.

5. After our two stories, I sent teams of students to sit together and take turns reading books using different voices for each character. Note: I preselected the book choices and paired my weakest readers with me.

Picture Books with Notable Voices:

- *Lilly's Purple Plastic Purse* by Kevin Henkes
- *No, David!* by David Shannon
- *That is Not a Good Idea!* by Mo Willems
- *The Day the Crayons Quit* by Drew Daywalt
- *The True Story of the Three Little Pigs* by Jon Scieszka
- *We Are in a Book!* by Mo Willems

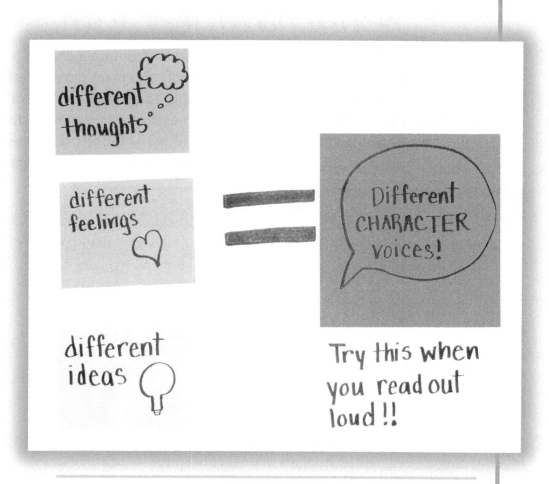

Figure 6.3 *Different Character Voices* chart

Informational Text Can . . .

The second grade informational text standard can be a challenge to teach. Students are asked to identify the main purpose of a text, including what the author wants to answer, explain, or describe. Personally, I find that a text can easily and frequently do all three: answer, explain, and describe. To make these categories more distinct, I created this chart with second graders.

Introducing This Chart:

1. I began by writing the title of the chart and drawing the pictures. After each picture, I added the category title and explained each one.

2. Then, I asked students to think of: (1) questions that they might have, (2) objects that they could describe, and (3) things that they could explain. We added these ideas to the list, again pointing out that these overlap.

3. Then, I held up three books and read the titles out loud: *Who Was Walt Disney?* by Whitney Stewart, *The Magic School Bus Lost in the Solar System* by Joanna Cole, and *How to Draw People* by Barbara Soloff Levy. I asked students to predict the purpose of each book. I deliberately selected books with titles that clearly implied that the book would answer a question, describe, or explain. Even with this careful selection, we still debated and I assured students that this was perfectly fine.

4. We ended the lesson with a brief summary and a reminder that informational text can have lots of different purposes.

Informational Text Can:

answer questions
- Where is Six Flags?
- Who is the president?
- Where is Florida?
- What day is Mother's Day on?

describe something
- Cheetah
- our school
- Grand Canyon
- president
- playground

explain things
- rules at school
- gravity
- roller-skating

Figure 6.4 *Informational Text Can . . .* chart

Readers Learn

During the first week of school, students learned to distinguish between literature and informational text. This simple chart, created during the second week of school, served as the introduction to informational text.

Introducing This Chart:

1. I gathered a collection of informational texts that contained lots of pictures with captions or callout boxes and several wordless books with only images. I sat students in teams of three and gave each team a different informational text.

2. I asked students to look through their books together and pay close attention to the pictures and the words.

3. After students had a few moments with their books, I drew the chart and talked about both parts. I asked students to raise their hands if they wanted to stand up and share something that a reader could learn from one of the pictures that they found. We continued sharing, then rotated the books around and repeated this cycle several times.

Informational Text with Multiple Images:

Asterisks indicate that there are additional informational texts written by the same author.

- *A Nest Full of Eggs* by Priscilla Belz Jenkins
- *Explore My World: Butterflies* by Marfé Ferguson Delano *
- *Explore My World: Penguins* by Jill Esbaum *
- *I Read Signs* by Tana Hoban
- *National Geographic Readers: Planets* by Elizabeth Carney *
- *National Geographic Readers: Weird Sea Creatures* by Laura Marsh*
- *Scholastic Readers: Seahorses* by Nicole Corse*
- *The Magic School Bus Takes a Moonwalk* by Joanna Cole *
- *Truck* by Donald Crews*

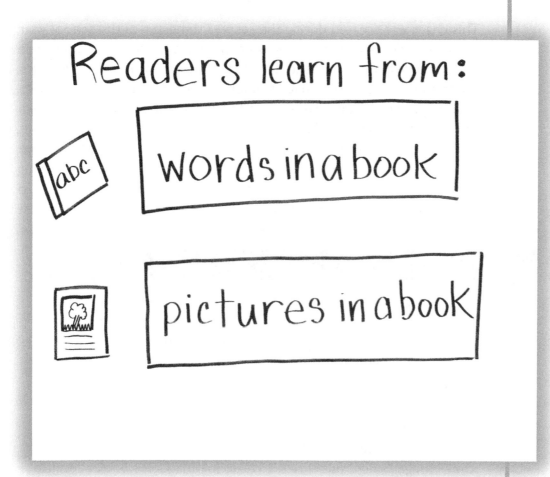

Figure 6.5 *Readers Learn* chart

Steps to Explain

This chart was created during the second semester of the school year, with students who had already been taught to identify the purpose of an informational text. This chart, created with second graders, goes a bit further than what the informational text standard requires. Second grade students are expected to identify the main purpose of a informational text, including what the author wants to answer, explain, or describe. This chart helps students to not just name the purpose, but to start forming paragraphs to explain their thinking. Teaching students to do this before they leave second grade is a great way to prepare them for the increased rigor of the third grade standards that require textual evidence and more complex explanations.

Writing Connection:

1. I read *The Magic School Bus Has a Heart* by Joanna Cole out loud to students. After reading, I asked students what they thought the purpose of the book was. We agreed that the book explained how the circulatory system worked.

2. After our discussion, I began to create the chart. As I explained each step, I also wrote a complete sentence for each one, thinking out loud about different ways to start my sentences.

3. Next, students were paired and asked to select a book from Joanna Cole's *Magic School Bus* series. I chose Joanna Cole's books because they are very similar and we had access to the Scholastic™ leveled-reading versions and the larger picture books.

4. When students had their selections, I asked them what the purpose of all of these books were. With prompting, we came to the conclusion that these books mostly explained science concepts. We acknowledged that you could make the case that they also described and answered questions.

5. Each student worked with a partner to read their selected book. When students finished, they followed the steps on the chart to write their own paragraphs that explained the purpose of the text.

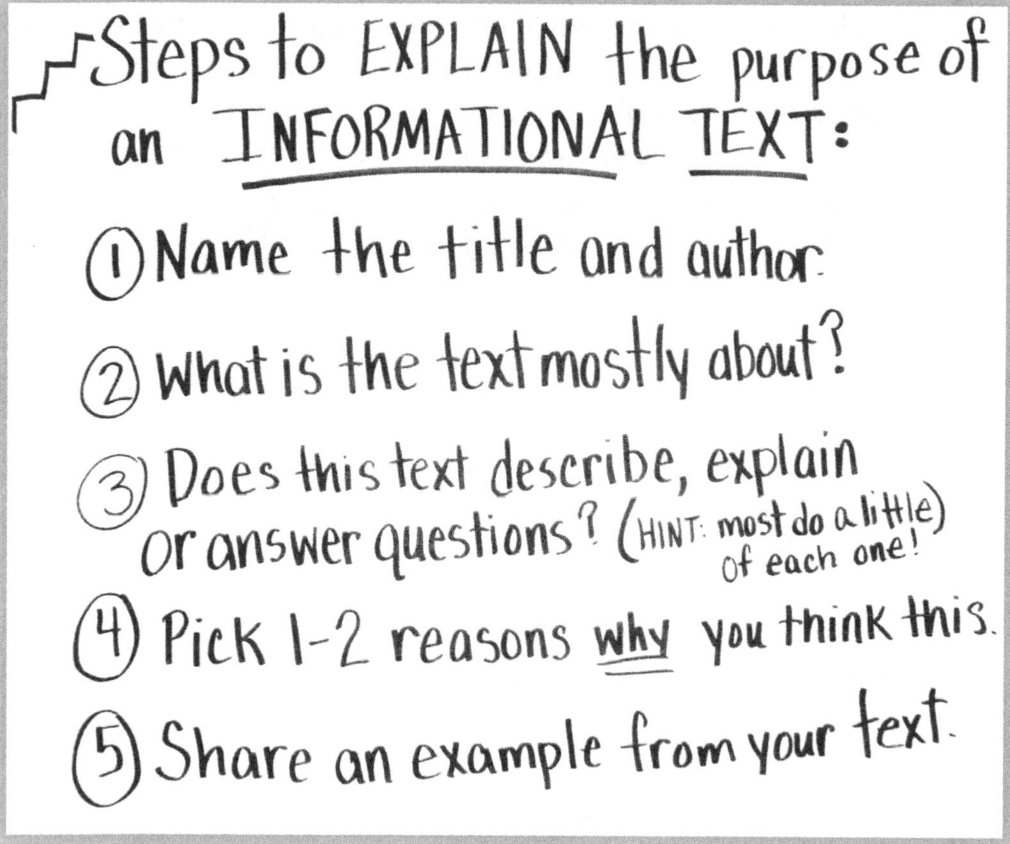

Steps to EXPLAIN the purpose of an INFORMATIONAL TEXT:

① Name the title and author.

② What is the text mostly about?

③ Does this text describe, explain or answer questions? (HINT: most do a little) of each one!

④ Pick 1-2 reasons _why_ you think this.

⑤ Share an example from your text.

Figure 6.6 *Steps to Explain* chart

We Work as a Team!

This chart was created with kindergarten students at the beginning of the school year. To introduce this effectively, you'll want to gather at least ten picture books. You won't need to read them right now, but you will want to show the book covers to students.

Introducing This Chart:

I gathered several books and held them up. I touched the title and the name of both the author and illustrator. When there was only one person serving as both author and illustrator, I pointed that out. After I read each book, I passed it to a student. The student could look at the book, read a page, or pass it on to another student. We repeated this several times. Finally, I told students to freeze. Each student that was holding one of the books came to the front of the class and held their book up. I called on students to either name the author or the illustrator. I did this repeatedly, and made it energetic and fun.

After we did this several times, I wrote the title and the names of the books on the chart. I held up each book listed on the chart and asked the students to tell me the title, author, and illustrator. When the students responded, I added the authors and illustrators to the chart.

Teaching Ideas:

- Consider photocopying the covers of the books that you plan to add to the chart. Attach these images to the chart instead of writing the titles.

- Mix in both literature and informational text. The standard is the same for both types of text. My chart did not include informational text, but easily could have.

- Send students in teams to look for books where the same person is both the author and illustrator. This could become a scavenger hunt and offer students lots of practice identifying authors and illustrators.

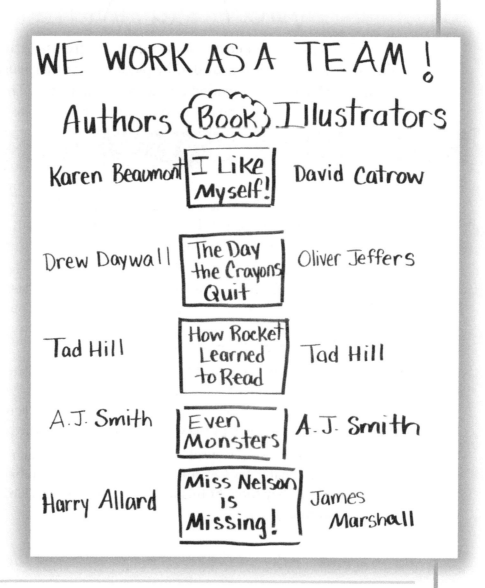

WE WORK AS A TEAM!

Authors (Book) Illustrators

Karen Beaumont	I Like Myself!	David Catrow
Drew Daywall	The Day the Crayons Quit	Oliver Jeffers
Tad Hill	How Rocket Learned to Read	Tad Hill
A.J. Smith	Even Monsters	A.J. Smith
Harry Allard	Miss Nelson is Missing!	James Marshall

Figure 6.7 *We Work as a Team!* chart

What Did We Learn?

The first grade informational text standard asks students to distinguish information provided by pictures or other illustrations from information provided by the words in a text. This simple chart encourages students to do just that.

Introducing This Chart:

1. I wrote the title on the chart and asked the students to tell me how we learn. I called on different students and prompted them toward the idea of learning from words and pictures. I added both of the terms and illustrations to the chart.

2. I told students that I thought we should test this out and see if we could really learn from both the images and the text. To "test" this out I asked students to listen as I read an informational text out loud. If they learned anything, they were to snap their fingers and explain whether they learned it from words, pictures, or both.

3. As I read *Smart Kids: Coral Reef* by Roger Priddy out loud, students snapped the whole time! Each time, I stopped and asked students not only what they learned, but whether it was from a picture or from just the words. Then, I placed some of the ideas on the chart.

4. When we finished, we reviewed our chart by reading each sticky note out loud. Finally, I asked students to give me a thumbs up or thumbs down if they thought this idea of learning from words and pictures was true.

Informational Text Series with Images and Words:

1. *DK Readers Series*

2. *National Geographic Readers Series*

3. *Scholastic Readers Series*

4. *Time for Kids (Science Scoop Series)*

What did we learn?

from the WORDS

from the PICTURES

from the WORDS	from the PICTURES
Snakes climb trees and swim.	Lionfish have stripes all over their bodies.
Sea Dragons are the slowest fish.	There are a lot of coral reefs!
Some fish lay 500 eggs at one time.	The Great Barrier Reef is shaped like a heart.

Figure 6.8 *What Did We Learn?* chart

Who Makes Books?

This simple chart was created with a group of kindergartners. Students are expected to recognize the roles of authors and illustrators. A large visual like this offers a simple reminder of the two roles.

Introducing This Chart:

1. To create this chart, I did an internet search for an image of an open book and sketched it out before I actually drew it with the students.

2. I showed students the image of the book, then asked what they thought I had drawn. Then, I added the title and asked: *Who makes books?* With kindergartners, I got the following responses: "teachers," "God," "the library," "Amazon," "people," and "nobody." After this creative medley of answers, I wrote the word *author* on the chart and had students say it with me.

3. We also repeated this same process for the *illustrator* part of the chart.

4. Finally, I asked students if they would rather be authors or illustrators. We ended our discussion with the promise that they would actually spend a lot of time this year being real authors and illustrators.

Teaching Ideas:

- Expand this chart to teach standards five and six by labeling the front and back covers as well.

- Let students use construction paper to create and label their own open books.

- Hold up different books, then call on students to name or point to the author's and/or illustrator's name.

- Share several books by Mo Willems or Dr. Seuss with your students Ask them why there is not a second name written on these books. *Did they forget to name the illustrator?* Explain that sometimes one person decides to write the words *and* draw the pictures in a book.

Figure 6.9 *Who Makes Books?* chart

Who Tells the Story?

This literature standard asks first graders to identify who is telling the story at different points in a text. To teach this effectively, you need literature with multiple narrators. One exception that I like to include when working on this standard is Eric Carle's *What's Your Favorite Animal?*. In this informational text, Carle has invited many well-known authors to tell readers what their favorite animals are. It is a great way to show that even though this is just one book, lots of people get to tell their own stories. For each chapter, the narration shifts. Because of this unique feature, I share this particular informational text with students alongside other literature selections.

Introducing This Chart:

1. I wrote the title on the chart and asked for responses to the question. Then, I told students that the narrator tells the story. This is the person that does the talking. Then, I added the 6"x4" sticky note to the chart that explains that.

2. Next, I read *What's Your Favorite Animal?* out loud. Every time a new narrator began a section, I stopped. We discussed the shift and added that person's name to the chart.

3. Over the course of two days, I read three additional books and we repeated this same process. The books that I read are all listed on the left side of this anchor chart. I did make sure to write all of the information on sticky notes so that the chart could be reused with other books throughout the year.

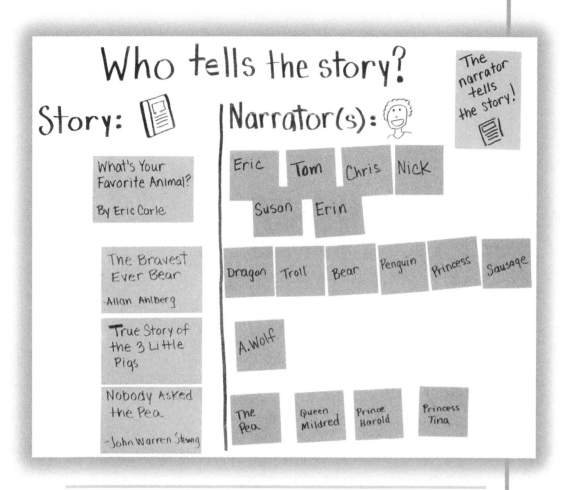

Who tells the story?

Story: 📖   **Narrator(s):** 🙂

The narrator tells the story! 📄

Story	Narrator(s)
What's Your Favorite Animal? By Eric Carle	Eric, Tom, Chris, Nick, Susan, Erin
The Bravest Ever Bear -Allan Ahlberg	Dragon, Troll, Bear, Penguin, Princess, Sausage
True Story of the 3 Little Pigs	A. Wolf
Nobody Asked the Pea -John Warren Stewig	The Pea, Queen Mildred, Prince Harold, Princess Tina

Figure 6.10 *Who Tells the Story?* chart

Chapter 7
Beyond Text

Common Core Reading Anchor Standard 7:
Integrate and evaluate content presented in diverse formats and media, including visually and quantitatively, as well as in words.

	Literary Text	Informational Text
K	*With prompting and support, describe the relationship between illustrations and the story in which they appear (e.g., what moment in a story an illustration depicts).*	*With prompting and support, describe the relationship between illustrations and the text in which they appear (e.g., what person, place, thing, or idea in the text an illustration depicts).*
1	*Use illustrations and details in a story to describe its characters, settings, or events.*	*Use the illustrations and details in a text to describe its key ideas.*
2	*Use information gained from the illustrations and words in a print or digital text to demonstrate understanding of its characters, setting, or plot.*	*Explain how specific images (e.g., a diagram showing how a machine works) contribute to and clarify a text.*

Books We Have Read

This informational text standard asks students to learn from images, illustrations, and the words in a text. To begin learning about books with different ways to gather information besides just text, I like to create this introductory chart with students to kick off this standard. This chart also ties in nicely with standard five. Both standards encourage students to pay closer attention to images and charts.

Creating This Chart:

I drew this chart from start to finish with my students. Then, I read *Maps and Globes* by Jack Knowlton out loud to them. After reading, I asked students if this book had any sentences. When they replied yes, I wrote the book title on a 4"x4" sticky note and placed it on the chart. Then I asked if the book had images. When students answered, I wrote the title on another sticky note and placed it on the chart. We repeated this for the last column as well. The next day, I read two more informational texts and we repeated this process again.

Teaching Ideas:

- Notice that I added a category for maps and charts. This overlaps with the learning from standard five. The content among standards will inevitably overlap, and so will your teaching; that's okay! If you really need or want to avoid this, create this same chart with only the first two columns, instead of all three.

- Treat this chart like a class reading log. Continue adding books throughout the year as evidence of not only the books that the class has read, but the different sources of learning within the books.

- Encourage students to share their own independent reading books that include images. Students could do this as the closing for a reading block or on predesignated days each week.

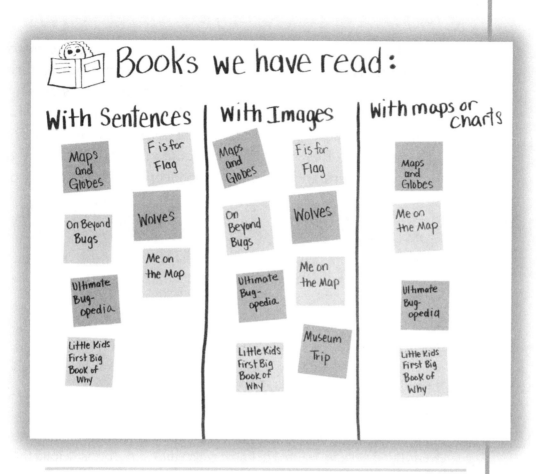

Figure 7.1 *Books We Have Read* chart

Characters, Settings, and Events

This chart addresses the second grade literature standard. Students are expected to use information from both pictures and words to understand and explain the characters, settings, and events. Students should already have been taught what characters, settings, and events are before you move to this standard. Revisit standard three if your students need to understand any of those concepts before moving on.

Introducing This Chart:

1. I wrote *characters, setting(s),* and *events* at the top of the chart and drew the pictures. I asked students to explain what they thought each word meant.

2. Next, I read *There Was an Old Lady Who Swallowed a Chick!* by Lucille Colandro. This book is an easy read and many second graders will have heard of this book before. I like to use familiar books when I first introduce this standard.

3. After reading this book, I added the words: *what we know* and *how we know.* I explained that I didn't just want to know who the characters were, but that I also wanted to know what clues in the book helped the students to understand the characters, settings, and events.

4. We moved from column to column adding what we knew and how we knew it.

5. After completing this chart, I asked students to select a partner and revisit a favorite book together. As they read, students were asked to talk about what they could learn from the pictures and the text.

6. Afterwards, we reconvened and shared some of the ways that we learned about the characters, settings, and events in our books.

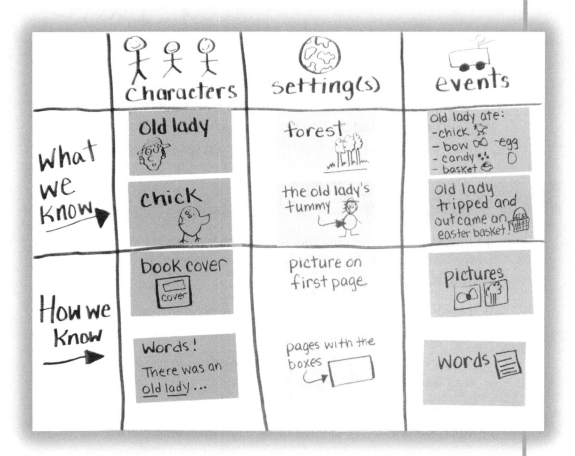

Figure 7.2 *Characters, Settings, and Events* chart

Key Ideas

The first grade informational text standard requires students to use the illustrations and details in a text to describe its key ideas. To introduce this standard, consider using your science or social studies books. Other good sources are almanacs and encyclopedia-style books. These types of books readily integrate text and images.

Introducing This Chart:

1. I drew the two columns and added both headings. I explained to the class that I wanted them to pay close attention to the pictures and the words as I read.

2. I read *Wolves* (out of print) by Michael Smith to the students. As I read, I stopped, asked questions, and pointed out different details.

3. When we finished reading, I asked students to share key ideas that they learned from the book.

4. As students shared, I wrote each of the key ideas on colorful 8"x6" sticky notes and placed them in the *Key Ideas* column.

5. Whenever a student shared a key idea, I called them to the front to show the page where they got that idea and to indicate if the idea came from an image or just the text. After our discussions, I wrote each response on a sticky note and placed it in the second column.

6. Each time a student shared, I tried to encourage a rich discussion about their key ideas. Sometimes I asked students to stand up, raise their hands, or move to different sides of the room based on whether or not they agreed. We continued most of our discussion in this manner.

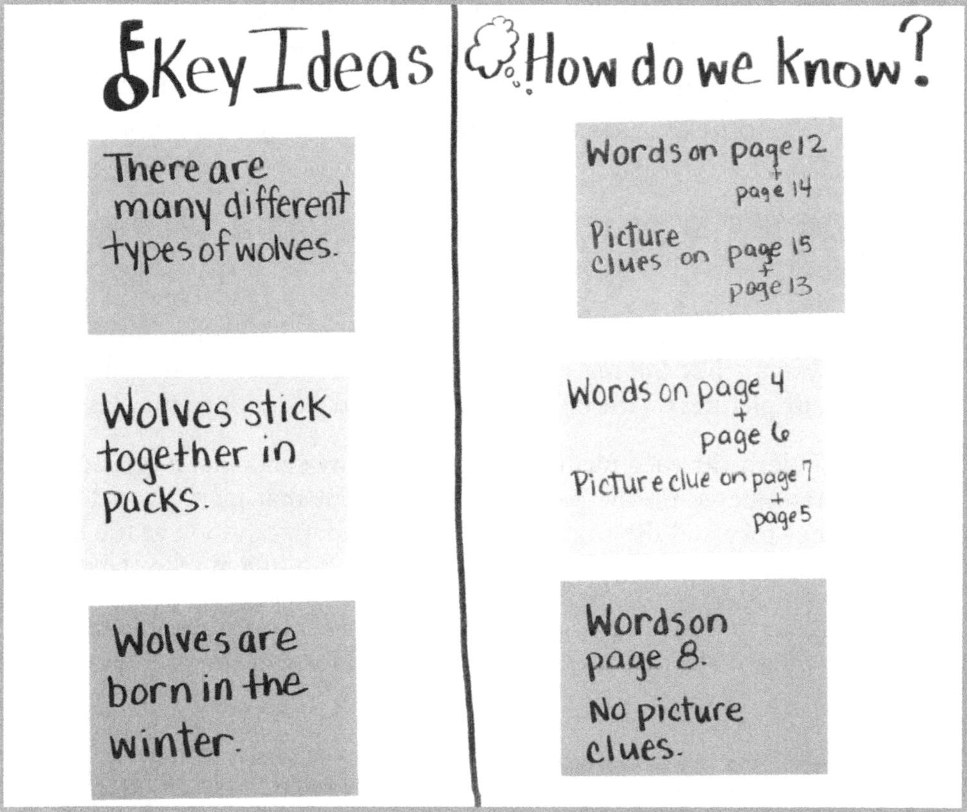

Key Ideas

Key Ideas	How do we know?
There are many different types of wolves.	Words on page 12 + page 14 Picture clues on page 15 + page 13
Wolves stick together in packs.	Words on page 4 + page 6 Picture clue on page 7 + page 5
Wolves are born in the winter.	Words on page 8. No picture clues.

Figure 7.3 *Key Ideas* chart

Let's Have a Picture Talk!

This literature standard asks kindergartners to describe the relationship between illustrations and the story in which they appear (e.g., what moment in a story an illustration depicts). To help students understand this, I like to draw four pictures that tell a story.

Introducing This Chart:

1. I gathered students on the carpet and read Jennifer Fosberry's *My Name is Not Isabella* out loud to the class. After reading, I drew the four pictures on the chart, then described each one to the class.

2. Underneath each picture, we wrote down events that happened in the story, based on the picture. I pointed out that pictures match up to the story and the words in the text. Readers can look at the different illustrations in a text and figure out what is happening in the story.

3. Then, I flipped back through the book and held up different illustrations. For each picture I asked students to describe what moment in the story the picture depicted.

4. Afterwards, I grouped students into groups of three and four. I assigned each group a couple of different books. I like to select predictable or wordless books for this activity, saving the more complex books for read-alouds. Students take turn "reading" the pictures and telling their partners what the image depicts.

Predictable or Wordless Books:

- *Brown Bear, Brown Bear* by Bill Martin and Eric Carle
- *Deep in the Forest* by Brinton Turkle
- *First Snow* by Emily Arnold McCully
- *Little Red Riding Hood* by John Goodall
- *Polar Bear, Polar Bear* by Bill Martin and Eric Carle

Let's Have a Picture Talk!

- Isabella would not answer to her name.

- Isabella pretended she was someone else!

- She was lots of famous women.

- She went on adventures.

- Mom stopped calling her Isabella (finally!)

- She decided to be herself again.

- She was proud to be Isabella.

Figure 7.4 *Let's Have a Picture Talk!* chart

Put All the Pieces Together

This simple chart serves as a reminder that readers use everything in the book to make meaning. I find that this is particularly useful for kindergarten students who are learning to decode at the same time. This chart reminds them that it is okay to rely on the pictures to understand the text.

Introducing This Chart:

1. I wrote the title at the top of the chart. Then, I explained that readers read more than just the words in a book. There are a lot of "pieces" involved in reading books.

2. I simply drew a box, then split it into four sections. I then wrote the word and drew the picture for each section. Once I completed a section of the puzzle, I held up a classroom example of each one.

3. For words, I used an alphabet card. For drawings, I held up one of the students' drawings. When I moved to photographs, I held up a picture of my daughter, then I pulled down the class map of America when I completed the maps section.

4. I have seen teachers get really creative here. Some teachers have not only held up a classroom example for each term, but asked students to draw each example. Others have taken photographs of each student and displayed them. Be as elaborate or creative as you can.

5. Note: maps are not a required part of this standard. Students can focus solely on photographs and illustrations. To include only three, draw your puzzle horizontally by drawing a rectangle and splitting it into thirds.

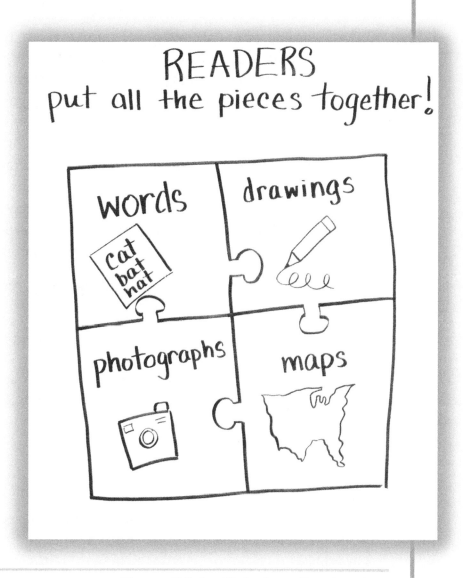

Figure 7.5 *Put All the Pieces Together* chart

Reading is About . . .

The wording of the second grade informational text standard is somewhat problematic; it reads: *Explain how specific images (e.g., a diagram showing how a machine works) contribute to and clarify a text.* The example of an image is a diagram. Typically, the standards name more than one example, but for this standard, there is only one example provided. This can be confusing because many teachers may take the word "image" literally and assume that this means pictures and photographs. "Images" is actually used as a proxy for multiple features. This chart is used to name specific types of images that students will encounter in text.

Creating This Chart:

I drew the title, face, and book on chart paper as students watched. When I finished, I wrote the names of different images on 6"x4" sticky notes. You can vary these names to be more specific, as needed. For example, I wrote *charts* on one sticky note. This could be broken up to include bar graphs, pie charts, etc.

Teaching Ideas:

- Read a book out loud that includes many of the features listed here before you create the chart.

- Ask students to locate these elements in other independent reading books or textbooks.

- Visit your school librarian and ask for a collection of books with different images. Assign one to each child in your class. Let students explore each book and add sticky notes on pages that contain different images.

Figure 7.6 *Reading is About . . .* chart

Chapter 8

Supporting Reasons

Common Core Reading Anchor Standard 8:
Delineate and evaluate the argument and specific claims in a text, including the validity of the reasoning as well as the relevance and sufficiency of the evidence.

	Literary Text	Informational Text
K	*(Not applicable to literature)*	*With prompting and support, identify the reasons an author gives to support points in a text.*
I	*(Not applicable to literature)*	*Identify the reasons an author gives to support points in a text.*
2	*(Not applicable to literature)*	*Describe how reasons support specific points the author makes in a text.*

Collecting Reasons

Reusable and fun to teach with, this chart supports the informational text standards for each grade level. Modify this, as needed, to meet the needs of different students.

Introducing This Chart:

1. I began by simply drawing the jar on this chart and reading an informational text to the class.

2. After reading the book out loud, I asked students what big point the author was making. With prompting, we decided on the main point and placed it at the top of the chart.

3. Then, I asked students to share fun and interesting facts that they learned from the text. I wrote each of these on 4"x4" sticky notes, placing them on the chart, outside of the jar.

4. Next, I called on students to come up to the chart and move sticky notes that supported the author's point into the jar. The class discussed whether each sentence really belonged in the jar or not. If it didn't, we moved it back out.

5. In the end, about half of the sentences were identified as supporting reasons. We repeated this activity with different informational texts.

My Informational Text:

If you are like me, you have accumulated lots of children's books over the years. The book that I used for this chart is one of those books. The students that I worked with were interested in wolves and coyotes. To build on that interest, I went through my library of books and came across a book called *Wolves* by Michael K. Smith. Later, when a colleague wanted to duplicate this lesson, I sent her the book title, only to find out that this book is no longer in print. With that said, if your students are interested in wolves, there are several interesting books written by Seymour Simon, Janni Howker, and Laura Marsh. Otherwise, any informational text can be used with this chart.

Figure 8.1 *Collecting Reasons* chart

Points and Reasons

This chart was created after reading Robert Cole's *The Story of Ruby Bridges*. This informational text is a Common Core read-aloud exemplar for second and third grade students. This chart is best for students who have already been introduced to reasons and points. If your students have not been introduced to these terms consider starting with the *What is a Point?* anchor chart first.

Introducing This Chart:

1. I created the headings and wrote the questions at the start of our reading block. Then, I introduced the book and shared some background information on Ruby Bridges.

2. After reading this book aloud, I put students in groups of five and asked them to talk about the key ideas or points that the author made. After about ten minutes of discussion in their small groups, I called the whole group back together.

3. As students shared different terms, we talked about each one and agreed on three major points that we felt were central to this text.

4. I wrote each of these on large 8"x6" sticky notes and placed them in the first column of the chart.

5. Then, I asked students to talk again in small groups about possible reasons to support these points. This time, when we reconvened, each group shared their ideas and we even reread some sections of the book.

6. We added several supporting reasons to the chart on smaller 4"x6" sticky notes. The following week, students repeated this process with other books.

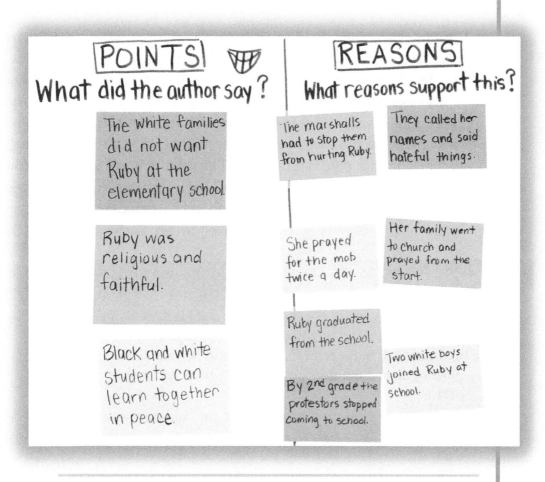

Figure 8.2 *Points and Reasons* chart

Straight to the Author's Point

This fun chart meets the demands of the informational text standard. Students are expected to understand that reasons support the author's points. The bullseye (center) is where the author's main point is placed. You can do this with the main point of an entire text, or the main point found within a paragraph. I initially found it confusing that the standards relied on the word *point.* After reading the standards vertically and working with different teachers, I learned that this is synonymous with what older students would call the author's *claim* or *argument.* Understanding this connection helped me to support students more effectively when teaching this standard.

Introducing This Chart:

1. I drew the target on the chart (there is a black dot underneath the sticky note in the center that makes the image look a bit more like a real target or bullseye). I asked students what this was. Amusingly, most of them identified the drawing as the logo for the Target® chain of stores.

2. I explained that the point is what the author wants readers to remember or learn. Then, I read *Throw Your Tooth on the Roof* by Selby Beeler. This text is listed as a Common Core exemplar for second and third grade students, but works just as well as a read aloud for kindergarten and first grade students.

3. After we read the book, we had a discussion about the big point of the book and added that to the center of the chart. Then, I had students share specific sentences that helped to prove the author's point. These supporting reasons were placed around the bullseye.

4. This chart can be used again by removing the sticky notes and replacing them with new ones when you read other books. Retire the old sticky notes to an unused corner of your room to reference later.

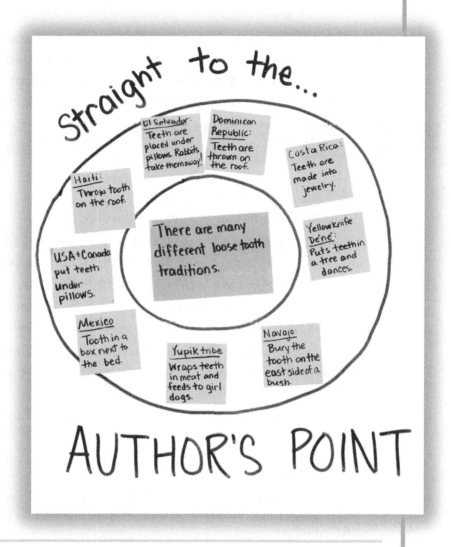

Figure 8.3 *Straight to the Author's Point* chart

What Do Reasons Really Do?

Teachers regularly ask students to find details and reasons in a text. While this request is valid, many students don't understand what really constitutes a concrete reason. The six ideas on this chart provide guidance to help students look for specific types of things.

Introducing This Chart:

1. I ask students to share what types of careers they want to have when they grow up. As students share, I write their ideas on the board. We spend about ten minutes discussing the different jobs.

2. Then, I shift gears and tell students that the sentences in books have jobs, too. I really ham it up and act like this is a big, important secret. *You guys didn't know that, did you? Oh, yeah, it's true!*

3. I lead a discussion about what possible jobs a sentence could have. Students get really silly and come up with all types of wacky ideas.

4. Finally, I tell students that in an informational text there are lots of sentences that support the main idea or point. These sentences are called reasons. Reasons can have six different jobs.

5. At this point I write the title on the chart and introduce each of the six "jobs."

Teaching Ideas:

1. Select six passages that feature each of the six types of reasons. Project each text on the whiteboard or read aloud to students as you introduce each "job."

2. Move directly into your science or social studies lesson after creating this chart. As you read text, stop at different sentences to ask students what job they think the sentence or sentences are taking on.

3. Send teams of students on a scavenger hunt to find sentences that function in these different roles. Reconvene as a whole group to share ideas.

4. Connect this to writing and have students craft sentences that explain, describe, or share examples.

Figure 8.4 *What Do Reasons Really Do?* chart

What is a Point?

The reading standards rely on the terms: *key ideas, main ideas,* and now *point* to indicate concepts that are very similar. The point is the claim or argument that the author is making. It is very likely that many of your students have never used the word *point* in this context. Begin instruction by teaching students what a point is. Later, students will be expected to read an informational text and decide what points and supporting reasons are included.

Creating This Chart:

1. To create this chart, I read the second grade standard out loud. Students seemed to understand most of the vocabulary; the notable exceptions were the words *reasons* and *point.* There was little consensus surrounding these two words.

2. I wrote the title on the chart and drew the speaking bubble. I told students that the text is just like the author talking to each and every one of us. The *point* is the big idea that the author wants to tell us about the topic.

3. After creating the speech bubble, I added the blocks underneath and explained that all of the other words are usually there to help support the author's point. As I explained these ideas, I completed the remainder of the chart.

Teaching Ideas:

- Create a graphic organizer modeled after this chart. Leave all of the words off. When students read an informational text, ask them to write the point in the speech bubble. Students can write the supporting reasons inside of each square.

- Compare looking for reasons to the way a detective looks for clues. Explain to students that they have to read closely and pay attention to words that appear frequently, ideas in bold or italic print, and headings to determine the author's point.

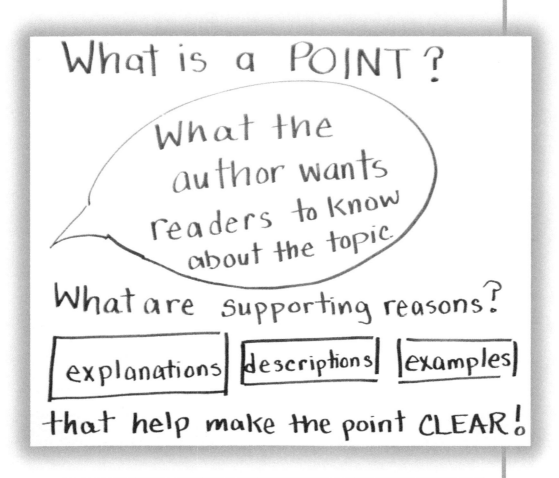

Figure 8.5 *What is a Point?* chart

Chapter 9
Multiple Texts

Common Core Reading Anchor Standard 9:
Analyze how two or more texts address similar themes or topics in order to build knowledge or to compare the approaches the authors take.

	Literary Text	**Informational Text**
K	*With prompting and support, compare and contrast the adventures and experiences of characters in familiar stories.*	*With prompting and support, identify basic similarities in and differences between two texts on the same topic (e.g., in illustrations, descriptions, or procedures).*
1	*Compare and contrast the adventures and experiences of characters in stories.*	*Identify basic similarities in and differences between two texts on the same topic (e.g., in illustrations, descriptions, or procedures).*
2	*Compare and contrast two or more versions of the same story (e.g., Cinderella stories) by different authors or from different cultures.*	*Compare and contrast the most important points presented by two texts on the same topic (e.g., in illustrations, descriptions, or procedures).*

Alike and Different

Let's talk about the elephant in the room: I draw really, *really* bad circles. Now that we've gotten that out of the way, let's dig into the meat of this chart. This chart supports the literature standard and can be used for any grade level. The goal is to help students to visualize how books are alike and different.

Grade Level Differences:

In kindergarten and first grade, the standard uses the terms "similarities and differences." In second grade, the language shifts to "compare and contrast." You can label your chart as I have done here or switch out the title to reflect the exact language used in the grade level that you teach.

Introducing This Chart:

1. For this lesson, I wrote the names of two Eric Carle books on the chart. I wrote the last words from each title on sticky notes just to make those stand out as the first real difference between the books. Then, I read both books out loud.

2. Afterwards, I wrote "brown bear" on a sticky note. I held it up and asked students which book included a brown bear. After I placed the sticky note on the *Brown Bear, Brown Bear, What Do You See?* side, I held up a second sticky note that read "hears a zookeeper." Students agreed that this belonged on the *Polar Bear, Polar Bear, What Do You Hear?* side.

3. I drew the Venn diagram circles around the sticky notes so that students could watch the two sides overlap.

4. Then, I explained that the space in the middle was for similarities. I continued to call on student volunteers to share similarities or differences, and I added these ideas to the chart.

5. When we finished the chart, I called on students to read some of the similarities and differences out loud.

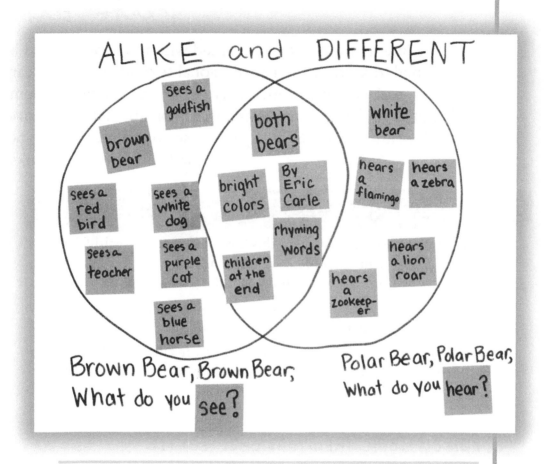

Figure 9.1 *Alike and Different* chart

Book Talk

This interactive chart was created with first graders and is designed to align to the informational text standard, but can easily be used with any type of book, story, or poem. The titles of the two books and the book characteristics are all written on 8"x6" sticky notes so that the chart can be reused with different books.

Teaching Ideas:

- Scaffold learning by using this chart to compare real-life objects. Compare items in your classroom, teachers, class pets, etc. Practice this a few times before shifting to full informational texts.

- Laminate this chart and reuse it with different books, or place in a center for students to use during center time.

- Consider creating this chart with literature after completing an author study. The class could compare and contrast books written by the same author.

Paired Topic Informational Texts:

1. *What's Out There?: A Book About Space* by Lynn Wilson & *Me and My Place in Space* by Joan Sweeney

2. *My First Biography: Benjamin Franklin* by Marion Dane Bauer & *Ben Franklin and His First Kite* by Stephen Krensky

3. *The Circulatory Story* by Mary Corcoran & *The Circulatory System* by Conrad Storad

4. *My First Biography: Martin Luther King, Jr.* by Marion Dane Bauer & *Martin's Big Words* by Doreen Rappaport

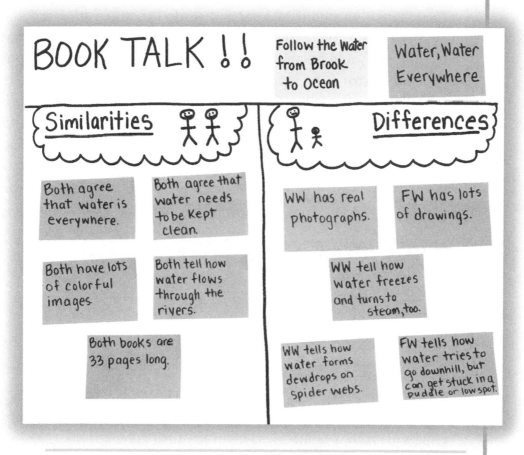

BOOK TALK !! Follow the Water from Brook to Ocean   Water, Water Everywhere

Similarities   **Differences**

Both agree that water is everywhere.

Both agree that water needs to be kept clean.

Both have lots of colorful images

Both tell how water flows through the rivers.

Both books are 33 pages long.

WW has real photographs.

FW has lots of drawings.

WW tell how water freezes and turns to steam, too.

WW tells how water forms dewdrops on spider webs.

FW tells how water tries to go downhill, but can get stuck in a puddle or low spot.

Figure 9.2 *Book Talk* chart

Cinderella Tales

This chart is aligned to the second grade literature standard and was really fun to create with students. The standard states that students should be able to compare and contrast two versions of the same story and actually names *Cinderella* as a possible text. There are so many great multicultural and even humorous versions of this classic tale. Other classic stories with multiple versions to consider: *The Three Little Pigs*, *Goldilocks*, and *Little Red Riding Hood*. For lots of teaching ideas and even more book lists visit *Read Write Think's* website: (http://www.readwritethink.org/files/resources/lesson_images/lesson853/FracturedFairyTalesBooklist.pdf)

Teaching Ideas:

- Switch out the large sticky notes and try different headings. Consider: problem, solution, message, or lesson.

- Read one book a day to build the chart over the course of a week. Use the last day of the week to write comparison and contrast sentences about the different books.

- Connect this chart to narrative writing. Ask students to write their own Cinderella stories. Students could share their narratives in small groups or create a similar chart to display their comparisons.

Ten Cinderella-Themed Picture Books:

1. *Adelita* by Tomie dePaola
2. *Cinder Edna* by Ellen Jackson
3. *Cinder Elly* by Frances Minters
4. *Cindy Ellen: A Wild West Cinderella* by Susan Lowell
5. *Mufaro's Beautiful Daughters* by John Steptoe
6. *Seriously, Cinderella is SO Annoying!* by Trisha Speed Shaskan
7. *The Egyptian Cinderella* by Shirley Climo
8. *The Gospel Cinderella* by Joyce Carol Thomas
9. *The Korean Cinderella* by Shirley Climo
10. *The Rough Face Girl* by Rafe Martin

Figure 9.3 *Cinderella Tales* chart

Compare

This chart was created with first graders and aligns to the literature standard. Students are expected to compare and contrast the adventures of characters in familiar stories. I read two books (that most students were already familiar with) out loud to the students. For our chart we reread *No David!* by David Shannon and *Llama llama and the Bully Goat* by Anna Dewdney.

Introducing This Chart:

1. After reading two different picture books, create the columns and write the word *compare* at the top of the chart. Ask students to name the main characters. Write these names at the top of each column or ask a student to do this.

2. Introduce each symbol and explain what each one means. The four categories that I included have no special magic. Use different categories or change them to meet the needs of your students. The goal is to get students talking about the characters and looking for similarities and differences. Other categories that I have used: *solution* (instead of fix-up), *adventures, experiences, inside* (for character emotions and feelings) and *outside* (for physical characteristics).

3. Once you have discussed each category, the fun can start! Lead a discussion about the characters with your students. Record their ideas and descriptions on the chart.

4. After creating this chart, ask students if they notice similarities or differences. Try to continue this rich discussion and encourage as many students as possible to share ideas.

5. I like to make this a permanent anchor chart in classrooms so that students can reference it. Other teachers prefer to reuse it with other characters, so they record all of the names and events on sticky notes.

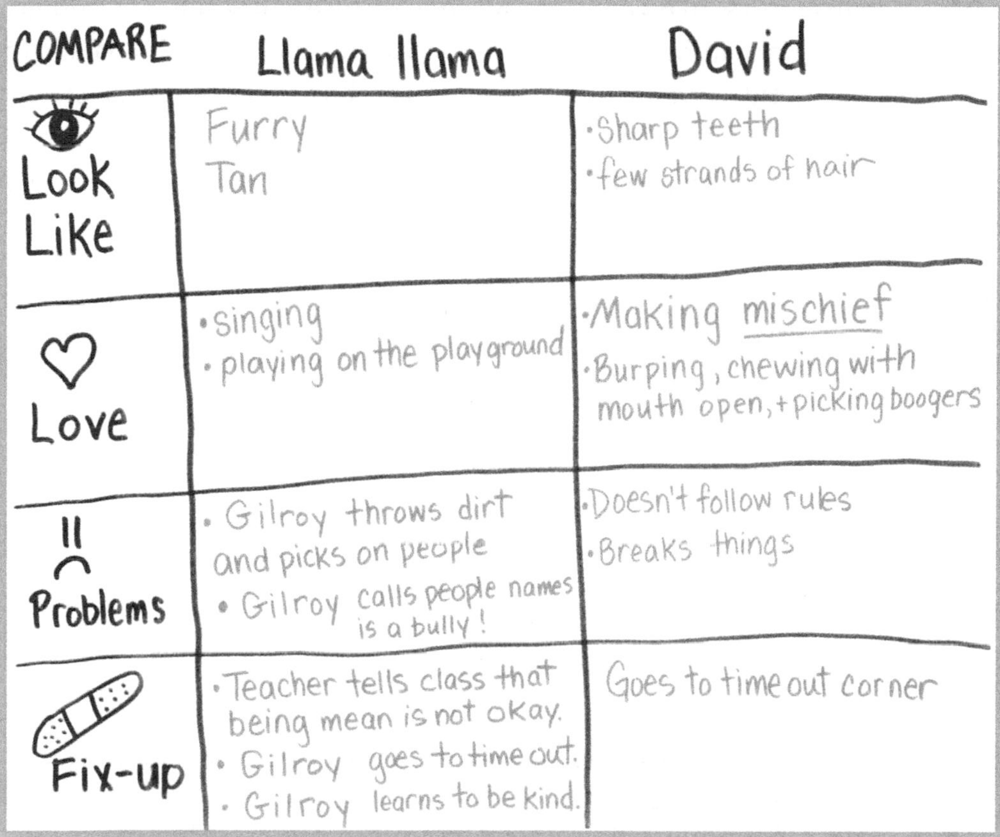

COMPARE	Llama llama	David
👁 Look Like	Furry Tan	•Sharp teeth •few strands of hair
♡ Love	•singing •playing on the playground	•Making mischief •Burping, chewing with mouth open, +picking boogers
⌒ Problems	•Gilroy throws dirt and picks on people •Gilroy calls people names is a bully!	•Doesn't follow rules •Breaks things
Fix-up	•Teacher tells class that being mean is not okay. •Gilroy goes to time out. •Gilroy learns to be kind.	Goes to time out corner

Figure 9.4 *Compare* chart

Comparing Texts

This interactive chart works well with the first and second grade informational text standard. To differentiate the chart, simply place different words in the middle. For this chart I have: *images, descriptions,* and *text structure.* These categories could be replaced with virtually anything that you are studying. You could even change them to story elements and use this chart with literature instead.

Introducing This Chart:

1. This chart was created with second graders. The students were studying Martin Luther King Jr.'s contributions to the Civil Rights Movement. Students had already read the Common Core exemplar, *Martin Luther King, Jr. and the March on Washington* by Frances Ruffin.

2. We began our discussion by summarizing Ruffin's text. Then, I told the students that today we would compare a second book about Dr. King. I asked students to think about the Ruffin version and see if they could find similarities and differences between the two books.

3. Next, I read *National Geographic's KIDS Martin Luther King, Jr.* by Kitson Jaznka out loud and begin to create the chart. We read each category: images, descriptions, and text structure (*text features* is an alternative term to use).

4. Then, I used a document camera to project excerpts from each book on the whiteboard. I called on different students to share differences and similarities as I wrote them down on sticky notes.

5. We used the author's initials to describe the similarities and differences. I really like to refer to what the author did, rather than what the book did. This helps students to think more like writers. *What did the writer do? How did this writer organize text?*

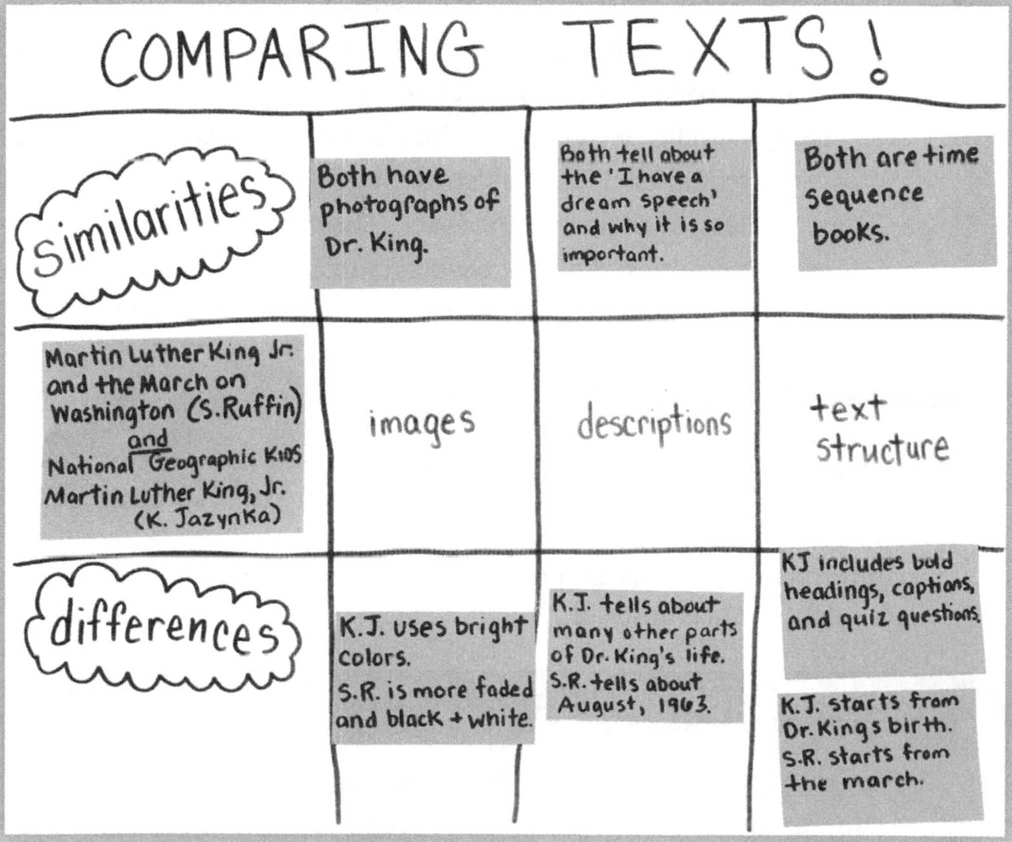

COMPARING TEXTS!

Similarities	Both have photographs of Dr. King.	Both tell about the 'I have a dream speech' and why it is so important.	Both are time sequence books.
Martin Luther King Jr. and the March on Washington (S. Ruffin) and National Geographic Kids Martin Luther King, Jr. (K. Jazynka)	images	descriptions	text structure
differences	K.J. uses bright colors. S.R. is more faded and black + white.	K.J. tells about many other parts of Dr. King's life. S.R. tells about August, 1963.	KJ includes bold headings, captions, and quiz questions. K.J. starts from Dr. Kings birth. S.R. starts from the march.

Figure 9.5 *Comparing Texts* chart

Such a Character!

This chart was created with first grade students and is appropriate for the literature standard. Students are asked to compare and contrast characters in stories. I deliberately select familiar, easy-to-read books when I first introduce skills to students. I want all students to have access to the skills, regardless of their reading level. The two stories that we read before creating this chart were Laura Numeroff's *If You Give a Dog a Donut* and *If You Give a Mouse Cookie*.

Creating This Chart:

I began by drawing the pictures of the dog and mouse on the chart. Students were tickled and curious. I am not an artist, so I stared at the cover of each book as I drew the animals on the front. If you are not comfortable doing this, try photocopying the book covers in advance and placing them here instead.

Teaching Ideas:

- Ask students to talk in small groups and identify the three most important or interesting parts from each story. Reconvene as a whole group to share ideas. Vote or raise hands to decide which events belong on the chart.

- Assign students to either the *dog* or *mouse* group. Let them create their own lists of the most important events. Ask each group to present their ideas to the whole class.

- Create this chart with your students, then select some of Laura Numeroff's other books to repeat this individually or in small groups.

- Consider asking students to write sentences that compare and contrast the adventures of both characters.

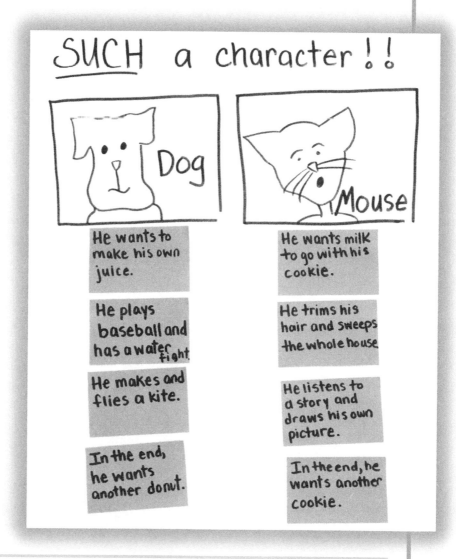

Figure 9.6 *Such a Character!* chart

Notes

Notes

Final Thoughts . . .

Whether you are a novice or a veteran teacher, I hope that **K-2 Chart Sense**™ has ignited a passion for using visual aids in the classroom. Visual aids, when created with your students, are meaningful and resonate with readers. Being an artist or creating the most colorful and attractive chart is never the focus. The goal is to create mental images that help readers. Obviously, you will not need every chart in this book, but I hope that the charts you create with your readers are powerful. Creating charts with your students not only strengthens your reading instruction, but inspires a strong sense of shared learning in your classroom. Ready to continue the conversation? Join me online at **www.rozlinder.com** for even more teaching ideas or to ask questions and collaborate. Happy reading!

Dr. Roz

ABOUT THE AUTHOR

Rozlyn Linder, Ph.D. is a dynamic and highly sought-after presenter, literacy consultant, and best-selling author. Known for her energetic, fast-paced seminars and workshops, she has traveled throughout the United States to collaborate with teachers at national and state conferences on literacy. An award-winning teacher, she has taught at all levels from elementary through college. She is passionate about motivating students through explicit instruction and the development of standards-based classrooms. Rozlyn and her husband, Chris, have two spirited daughters.

CPSIA information can be obtained at www.ICGtesting.com
Printed in the USA
LVOW03s0120151014

408810LV00006B/93/P